WHATEVER H. TO SIN?

*Virtue, Friendship and Happiness
In the Moral Life*

Charles E. Bouchard, O.P.

NEW PRIORY PRESS
EXPLORING THE DOMINICAN VISION

Published by New Priory Press
2005 South Ashland Avenue, Chicago, IL 60608-2903
NewPrioryPress.com

Cover Design: Susan Webb

Cover Art: The Virtue of Prudence, Amiens Cathedral, west entrance.

Contents

Introduction

Morality is a tough subject. Many people see it as a dismal science, all about obligations and prohibitions and suffering. They may reject it out of hand because it fails to answer the questions they are asking. Others see it as the realm of experts and don't think they have the tools to make "ethical" decisions. Morality it is full of controversy, since every person has to make moral choices and sometimes one person's judgments conflicts with another's. In one sense, everyone is a moral theologian.

This book is designed to take some of the terror out of morality. It is written for adult Catholics who got some of the conclusions about the moral life (mostly in the form of "thou shall nots,"[1]) but who may not have gotten a clear understanding of the "why" of the moral life.

This book is based on three basic assumptions. First of all, it assumes that morality is a creative endeavor; far from being only about prohibitions, the moral life is the result of our search for happiness and fulfillment.

Second, the moral life is not just about what we *do*, but about what kinds of persons we want to *be*. Moral choices may start with "doing", but they quickly evolve into "being." What we do makes us who we are, and who we are determines what we choose to do in the future.

Finally, morality is essentially a social undertaking. It is true that morality involves individual moral choices and personal responsibility, but ultimately the goal of the moral life is the good of the group – whether it be the family, the community or the world. We acquire virtue through our moral choices but we cannot do this apart from our relationships. Our relationships influence our choices and our choices affect our relationships. This makes friendship an important aspect of the moral life.

This book is the fruit of many years of teaching moral theology to undergraduates, graduate theology students and seminarians. One of my greatest pleasures was to help them see morality in a new way and help them embrace it as the most important task of their lives. I thank them for all I learned from them.

PART I: MORALITY BECOMES CHRISTIAN

Chapter I – The Changing Shape of Christian Morality

It seems like every day's newspaper carries another story of a problem in ethics: legal ethics surrounding a bribery or political scandal; medical ethics concerning organ donation, surrogate motherhood, or physician-assisted suicide; or business ethics, when a corporation violates its public trust or makes questionable profits. We are sometimes left with the impression that ethics is a twentieth century invention and that life in past times must have been simpler and less fraught with dangers.

In some ways, that is surely true. Before highly advanced medicine, multi-national corporations or vast, televised election campaigns, life was simpler and so were the ethical problems people faced. But every generation has coped with what it means to be moral, and each generation has had to work out specific answers anew. There are constants in our ethical tradition, but the detailed answers to specific questions require perceptive eyes and careful thought. While it might be true to say that ethical values are universal and unchanging, the norms which articulate them and reveal them to us change a great deal depending on the society, times and circumstances in which we live.

The Catholic tradition in morality is strong and dynamic. We can trace themes and principles which have remained constant almost from the beginning, but we can also see flexibility and accommodation as it responded to real changes in society and history.

1

The Emergence of Christian Morality:
The Patristic Period, A.D. 100-400

The earliest Christians lacked an identity of their own. Only gradually did they discover what it meant to be a church, or a community of those whose belief in Jesus made them different. Many early Christians expected Jesus to return sooner rather than later, and they did not see a highly developed moral system as important. Their morality was more a question of "living together until Jesus returns," so moral instruction was informal, pragmatic and uncomplicated. Early Christianity was a variety of Judaism, so early Christian morality resembled traditional Jewish morality more than anything else. As missionaries spread out and began converting non-Jewish Greeks and Romans, they brought their moral traditions (derived from classical philosophy) with them and the emerging Christian tradition blended them in, as well. This is precisely what was at issue when Peter baptizes Cornelius, a Gentile, in Chapter 10 of the Acts of the Apostles. After doing so, his Peter's Jewish associates were shocked at his "immoral" association with a non-Jew. Peter receives a vision instructing him to eat meat traditionally forbidden to Jews, and God's voice says, "What God has purified you are not to call unclean." Peter realized that this meant that traditional Jewish law could be bent for the sake of bringing Gentiles into the Christian fold. Elsewhere, St. Paul instructs Gentiles only to refrain from the meat of strangled animals, thus relaxing the traditional Jewish requirements. As Christianity expanded, it gradually developed its own ethic and its own moral structure.

Even into the second and third centuries, however, Christian morality remained informal and relatively unorganized; early Christian thinkers might be said to have "made it up as they went along," since they faced moral questions as they arose and did not try to construct a systematic program of ethics. This approach was often exemplified by writers who wrote treatises on various topics which were bothering earlier Christians. One such was entitled "Whether the Rich May be Saved," written by Clement of Alexandria in the second century. More and more Christian converts were prosperous, and the church was trying to figure out how to reconcile this with Jesus' exhortation to poverty, and specifically with the passage "It is easier for a camel to pass through the eye of a needle..." Many felt that this made it impossible for the wealthy to be Christian. In a subtle interpretation of the Scriptural witness, Clement said it was not what one owns so much as how one uses it, and that the both poor and wealthy alike must remember that they have responsibilities to one another: the rich to provide for the material needs of the poor, and the poor to preach the Gospel to the rich.

The moral literature of the time was often rich in symbolism and allegory which made it appealing and easy to remember. The Shepherd of Hermas, who wrote about the year 200, dealt with another specific problem which arose from the fact that confession as we know it today did not yet exist, and people were often only able to receive forgiveness once, at baptism. What happens, he asked, to those who sinned after Baptism? Were they lost forever? Like Clement, The Shepherd deals delicately with this problem, but allows that there may be one more reconciliation after Baptism, which should not be taken lightly. He uses colorful images of the church as an old woman growing younger (regenerated by penance), the church as a tower reaching to heaven, built of rocks (the faithful) taken from the stream (of Baptism). These images stuck in the minds of listeners and helped them to absorb the emerging doctrine of sin and reconciliation.

Other early sources, like the first century *Didache* presented Christian morality as a choice between two "ways," the way of Life and the way of Death. Yet it allowed that there would be those who could not accept "the Lord's yoke in its entirety," and they should "do what they could..." Much of the specific moral content of this document was simple common sense and was drawn from the prevailing secular ethics: shun evil, avoid anger, do not be fanatical, do not be a grumbler. Other ideas, like the prohibition of fortune telling and augury, reflected fascination with such things among early Christians.

After St. Paul himself, St. Augustine was probably the Church's first real moral theologian. But as was the case with most patristic moralists, his works, too, were occasioned by specific controversies, questions and disputes, not the least of which was his own struggle with sexual immorality. Yet his elaborate writings on sin, grace, and conversion became a rich source to which subsequent writers would return century after century.

Private Confession and the Penitentials: 400-1000 a.d.

Unfortunately, Augustine wrote just at the close of the Church's earliest period of development. The fall of the Roman Empire, the Barbarian invasions from the north and other cultural events pretty much "turned out the lights" on theological speculation and inquiry for several centuries. Although the years between 400 and 1100 are often referred to as the Dark Ages because there was little public intellectual or theological activity, the moral tradition of the church continued to grow in monasteries and through private moral direction provided by monks to one another and to the laity who came to their doors.

This private moral counsel, which was the forerunner of modern day "confession," gave rise to a whole genre of literature called the *penitentials.*[2] These were lists of penances to be assigned for various sins, and they give us a graphic picture of what daily life was like in this era, as well as how the church once again adapted itself to changing cultural and historical circumstances. The penitentials speak of the usual sins like theft, lying, fornication, pride and anger; but they also treat more exotic sins like bestiality, desecration of the consecrated host, incest, and pedophilia. In each case, the writers carefully distinguished the age, mental ability and social status of the sinner and tried to provide an appropriate penance. Unlike recent times, however, penances were not seen as punishment for sin, but rather as "healing medicine," which the priest (or lay monk, since these penances were not yet "sacramental" in our sense of the word and were often celebrated by the laity) administered much as a physician would for a sick patient. One writer, in words that are still good advice for confessors today, writes:

> "Let the power of the physician became greater in the degree in which the fever of the sick man increases. Those who take care the heal the [spiritual] wounds of others are to observe carefully what is the age and sex of the sinner, what instruction he has received, what is his strength, how long he has remained in sinful delight..."

The penitentials marked a departure from the highly social and communal nature of moral discipline in the early church. We have already noted that for the first few generations of Church history, reconciliation was only available once; later, it became available somewhat more frequently, but was usually public and communal in nature. Those who had sinned seriously, for example, were required to do "public penance," which might involve distinctive dress, banishment or fasting which would mark one as a sinner begging the community's forgiveness. These sinners would be reconciled as a group during the Easter vigil.

As the church grew and as early Christian idealism faded, communities began to realize that the church could not be fully purged of sin until Jesus' triumphant return. The penitentials signaled a move from infrequent, rigorous, public reconciliation, to private, personal confession which acknowledged the fact that people sin repeatedly and that moral conversion is an ongoing process rather than a dramatic, once-and-for-all event. As a matter of convenience and in order to lessen the embarrassment of public penance, the priest came to stand in for the community as a whole, and he, rather than the community, became the agent of God's forgiving power.

The penitentials began in Irish monasteries, but soon spread all over Europe as Irish monks went to Britain, France, Germany and Spain as missionaries. Although some historians are skeptical about the origin of these books (one says that many of the cases found there are surely "webs spun in the casuistry of the monkish brain...thought up in the cloister by the tortuous intellect of the clerical scribe"), there is no doubt in my mind that they are relatively accurate representations of the moral problems which plagued the church in these ages, and that they describe a real effort on the church's part to continue providing pastoral care even when cities, churches and centers of learning had been debilitated.

In our own age, we have drawn a sharp line between "morality", which we often identify with law and obligation, and "spirituality" which understand as having to do with prayer, the virtues, and our sacramental lives. Throughout both the patristic and penitential periods, however, no such distinction existed. Morality and spirituality – behavior and prayer, body and soul – were of a piece. So St. Paul, St. Clement of Alexandria, St. Augustine and the writers of the penitentials would never have thought of placing morality in a separate category. For them, "morality" was simply the way in which Christians properly lived their lives, that could not be separated from how they prayed, or worshipped or "believed." In fact, it has been said that one of the reasons moral theology is so contentious is that "everyone is a moral theologian." This means that as soon as we make an act of faith in Jesus, we have to then begin to deliberate about how that faith affects the way we live. That is precisely what "morality" (or religious ethics) is. It is the search for a kind of behavior which is consistent with our faith.

The Systematic Development of Catholic Morality: 1200-1600

We have spoken of the "Dark Ages" as a period of cultural recovery, when intellectual and spiritual activity was quiet and largely hidden in the great monasteries of Europe. Although important advances were being made in pastoral care and moral theology, there were few means of communication, so very little information or thought was shared.

Like a sleeping bear awakening after a long hibernation, and for reasons not entirely understood, Europe awoke from its six-century long cultural and intellectual sleep early in the 13th century. The so-called "Middle Ages" followed centuries of quiet agrarian life with little theological activity and were marked by the sudden and dramatic rise of great urban centers and an explosion of artistic and intellectual activity. Most of the great Universities of Europe were founded in this period, and most of the great cathedrals – Chartres, Notre Dame, Salisbury, were begun.

As cities grew and flourished and more and more people moved from the quiet life of the farm to expanding urban centers, the Church realized that the quiet pastoral spirit of the penitentials, which had been the primary vehicle for moral instruction from the 5th through the 10th centuries, was no longer adequate. Urban life presented a whole array of new moral problems, not the least of which was the reappearance of dualistic and gnostic heresies like Albigensianism which denied the goodness of created reality and established secret and exclusive societies which were at odds with Christian life. The medieval cathedrals, with their colorful windows and sculpture depicting the virtues and vices, the Ten Commandments, and important saints and feasts in the Church year, were a partial solution to the need for greater moral catechesis. The mendicant, or "begging" orders like the Dominicans and Franciscans were founded to provide preachers who could travel from town to town rather than stay put in their rural monasteries, were another way of meeting the need for education.

Faculties of theology developed, and theologians such as St. Thomas Aquinas, St. Bonaventure and many others wrote great synthetic works of theology which tried to blend traditional Christian sources with new insights received from Aristotle and other ancient Greek philosophers. These thinkers, who stressed the need to train human ability for life in tightly knit cities of ancient Greece, provided the perfect basis for moral and political life in the rapidly developing cities of medieval Europe.

In morality, this resulted in a highly sophisticated picture of the human person shaped by moral virtues – skills which are acquired by practice and begin to shape future behavior. Eventually, virtue shapes individual acts into inclinations to act in a certain way and an identifiable moral character begins to emerge. We experience the fact of moral character intuitively every time we make a judgment about someone's reliability, truthfulness or integrity. The fact that we can predict, to some extent, whether someone we know will tell the truth, finish the job, act charitably, cheat or deceive indicate that we all have virtues – or vices – which shape our actions.

We speak of a *virtuoso* as someone who is unusually and naturally talented. Much like the skills of a talented violinist, the virtues of prudence, temperance, fortitude and justice shape moral ability and enable us to make good moral choices naturally and easily. Prudence, keystone of all the virtues, is the ability to deliberate and choose well. Prudent persons those who can naturally "do the right thing," those who seem to have an unusual ability to see reality as it is was, and consistently weigh advantages and disadvantages of various choices to choose what was best in the long run.

Justice is the virtue governing the equitable allocation of goods, and enables one to "give each his or her due." *Temperance* governs the human need for comfort and pleasure and enables us to seek the right amount – neither too much nor too little. The temperate person would know how much tasty food was reasonable, for example, and would avoid both gluttony and excessive fasting. It avoids vices of overindulgence and "insensibility" – the abnormal loss of all ability to enjoy pleasure.

Finally, *fortitude* is the virtue governing fear; it enables one to face obstacles to good choices courageously and overcome them. The mother who defends her children against danger and the judge who pronounces truly just decisions despite opposition, for example, both act out of fortitude.

Together, the virtues describe what it is like to be fully human, to fully realize human capacities for pleasure, courage, intelligence and life in community. They are, as we often say, "their own reward," because just as the master violinist receives pleasure from playing the violin, so the virtuous person learns to "play" his personality to the fullest and experience moral and spiritual harmony. The truly virtuous person is someone who has trained her various human abilities to work together so that – much as a finely engineered and well-tuned machine – there is a minimum of conflict and malfunction.

Sin was the deliberate choice of a lesser good, one which was not fully human. "Vice," the opposite of virtue, was the acquired inclination toward sinful acts. Much as a poorly taught violinist consistently plays poorly, the "vicious" person is one who deliberately choses poorly again and again until the tendency to do so is deeply rooted and begins to influence future choices. Vice is a "bad habit" – not in the sense of an unconscious action like chewing one's fingernails, but in the sense of an inclination toward less-than-fulfilling, or sinful, choices.

The Legalization of Moral Theology: 1500-1965

Since there was no established seminary system at the time, the education of the clergy was unsystematic and often woefully inadequate. In the 15th century, for example, investigators discovered priests who did not know how many sacraments there were and who were using the "Hail Mary" in place of a formula of absolution for confession. Although priests who aspired to university teaching (often members of religious orders such as Dominicans and Franciscans) received a university education, most of the clergy engaged in pastoral care received their training through apprenticeship to older priests and they were often not theologically prepared to answer the challenges of the heretical sects.

By the 16th century the problem had grown so great that the Fathers of the Council of Trent inaugurated a comprehensive program of studies for priesthood students based on the "short course" developed by the recently founded Society of Jesus for seminarians who would deliver pastoral care rather than become university professors. This represented a vast improvement over the hodge-podge of education which priests received prior to this time, but the short course was geared to pastoral care, and was shaped by the growing practice of individual confession, which had not existed widely until now. The Council Fathers were eager to assure that there was a regularized confessional discipline, so that priests everywhere understood relative gravity of sin in the same way. Thus, after the 16th century priests were trained primarily to determine two things: First, was there sin present in the penitent's confession; and secondly, if so, how serious was it? Although this approach had the admirable purpose of making the penitent's moral burden as light as possible by not requiring too much, it also shifted the primary understanding of what morality really was.

While through most of the church's history morality was seen as the acquisition of virtue – skills for living rightly – the emphasis after the council of Trent fell on avoiding sin. It was a subtle shift, but had wide reaching ramifications. Increasingly, morality became identified with sin, and the positive emphasis which virtue theory brought to the moral life faded from view. Instead of guiding people toward realization of the fullness of human capacities, morality took on the appearance of a law book and asked only whether sin was present. Eventually, the virtuous life became almost solely the domain of priests and religious who had the time to pursue such activities. The average lay person had to be content with merely avoiding sin and doing the minimum required by the law.

The moral literature of the period, the *manuals,* imitated the legal books of the time. They were highly codified and schematic, and carefully distinguished kinds and levels of sin. Although geared to helping confessors accurately identify and absolve sins, they omitted the "heart" of the moral life and made morality look like a game of legal hide-and-seek. Many of the faithful lost sight of moral continuity, were unable to see morality as having anything to do with a good human life or the cooperation of human ability with grace. They came to see it almost exclusively in terms of discrete acts and obedience to the law.

For a variety of reasons, this legalistic understanding of morality – which made "moral" the equivalent of "legal", became deeply entrenched and lasted well into the 20th century. But it was a relatively

9

late development and did not capture the fullness of the Catholic moral tradition. In time, the manual tradition, complex and detailed as it was, became brittle and unresponsive.

In the early 1960s the Second Vatican Council recognized this and urged a renewal of moral theology. The manuals, which had been the sole textbooks of morality for over three centuries, disappeared almost overnight. Although they had achieved an astonishing degree of conciseness and clarity, their main purpose, to help clergy to determine the presence of sin, was inadequate for a changing church.

The disappearance of the manuals, whose codified and legalistic method had become synonymous with moral theology over the centuries, created a huge vacuum in the study of morality. Although the Redemptorist moral theologian Bernard Häring tried to bridge the gap with his three volume series *The Law of Christ* in the early 1960s, this proved inadequate and he wrote another series, *Free and Faithful in Christ* several years later. There were few textbooks, and many professors of moral theology resorted to their own notes or article. Standardized textbooks only began to reappear in the early 1980s.

This period of transition created a great deal of confusion for Catholics who had learned to identify morality with legal obligation. They felt angry that laws and rules with which they had been so familiar during their childhood were now being abandoned or modified almost daily.

The problem was that most of these rules (e.g., abstinence from meat on Friday) were never really a matter of morality, but of church discipline. They should never have been so tightly linked with morality. The importance that was given to these rules displaced and trivialized important moral matters like growth in good judgment and understanding of the values behind moral teachings. Though it may have seemed that morality was going down the drain, all that was happening was a normal adjustment not unlike many others which had been made in the course of church history. Just as changing times required that the church shift from the kind of informal morality which characterized the early church to the more detailed approach of the penitentials, so the twentieth century required a move away from the schematic approach of the manuals to one which was more cognizant of psychology and moral development.

What Does Moral Theology Look Like Today?

The moral theology we had up until the Second Vatican Council in 1963 was the result of several hundred years of development, so it should come as no surprise that a new paradigm or a new model for the moral catechesis will take a long time to evolve fully. Many of the basic elements of Catholic morality, which we will describe in the first part of this book, have remained constant. It is only the way we teach and appropriate them that has changed. Yet, from one historical period to another there are changes in emphasis. Some aspects of our moral tradition have become less prominent and others have taken on a new vitality. Let me briefly describe some of those that have become more important in the last generation or two.

The most important development is a rediscovery of the *role of the Holy Spirit* in the moral life. As we shall see in Chapter 14, the Spirit was neglected in favor of more juridical and canonical aspects of the morality. The Spirit became suspect because the kind of interiority it fostered appeared to be at odds with the external obligations imposed by the law. Happily, the Spirit is making a comeback and we are rediscovering how it energizes and completes our moral pursuits.

Closely related to this is the rediscovery of the *relationship among morality, liturgy and spirituality*. In fact, I shall maintain that properly understood, morality and spirituality are essentially the same thing and they are both nourished by liturgy and preaching.

Scripture has also found a new home in moral theology. While it was often only used to proof-text conclusions derived in other ways, today Scripture is a starting point for moral reflection. We have learned to look to the Bible as a primary source of moral inspiration.

The *re-emergence of virtue* as the core of the moral life is another important development. For many centuries morality was understood primarily in terms of obligation; virtue and affect received little attention. Today we are retrieving the tradition of Aristotle, Augustine and St. Thomas Aquinas for whom virtue was the heart of ethics. Virtue-based ethics requires a far more complex understanding of the human person, but it is also richer and more satisfying than a merely legal approach.

Dialogue between psychology and morality is another important development. It is true that in some ways our society is over-psychologized. It is also true that there are dangers to an overly psychological approach to morality which places too much emphasis on subjective factors. But our understanding of psychology and the emotions have given us important insights into moral decision-making and human freedom.

Finally, *publicity* has made a huge difference. In the past, sensitive moral issues were discussed only by clerics, in Latin, in moral theology textbooks. Few laymen were even part of the conversation. Today, many sophisticated moral issues are not only discussed, but argued in public. Economic, sexual, medical military and legal questions in ethics are analyzed on the front page of newspapers, in blogs and on television. This has made moral theology much more democratic. It has also given rise to new questions in ethics that our forebears would never have imagined.

Two important lessons are apparent from this overview of the development of Christian morality. First of all, as early Christian thinkers showed, we must not be afraid to find answers to new moral dilemmas as they arise. Just as St. Clement realized that wealth posed a problem for early Christians who took Jesus' words seriously, so later thinkers realized that war, interest on loans, slavery, medical technology and AIDS pose problems which simply did not exist in previous generations and which were not addressed in Scripture. The genius of the Catholic moral tradition is its ability to face new questions and search out answers to them.

Second, the history of moral theology reminds us that we must seek out moral wisdom wherever it is found. Since Scripture does not address every moral dilemma, we are sometimes left to look elsewhere, including to common sense, for answers. Because we believe that grace flows through human history, intelligence and experience as well as through Scripture and revelation, we should not be afraid to look around us. This is precisely what St. Paul and the early Church fathers did as they gleaned moral wisdom from Greek philosophy, Jewish life, and secular literature. In a similar way, St. Thomas Aquinas drew on the prevailing philosophical wisdom of his day, and appropriated the thought of the philosopher Aristotle. For us today modern science, popular culture, history, literature and the social sciences can all provide glimmers of wisdom and grace which we can confidently use to chart a moral course.

Chapter 2 – How Catholics Make Moral Decisions

Although the development of Christian morality has its own distinct history, it is part of a larger picture which includes many other ways of making moral decisions. Let us look at each of a number of possibilities, and then locate the Catholic approach among them.

Morality as a Particular Kind of Knowing

When someone says "two plus two equals four," anyone who understands the terms knows the truth of the statement. This kind of knowledge is straightforward and doesn't admit of much dispute or argument. Moral knowledge – the kind involved in a statement like "you ought to do this" is of another sort, however. Although it does have an objective dimension to it, (that is, it is not merely opinion) it is much more flexible and often admits of argument or even controversy. In many cases, when someone says "That is immoral," there are five other people who are willing to say "That is not immoral," or "it depends." Even at its best morality is an imprecise science because it deals with human behavior rather than with hard scientific facts or abstract theory.

Kinds of Moral Decision Making

The fact that human persons are made in the image of God means they are blessed with intelligence and reason. This enables them to make moral decisions. We must decide whether to lie or tell the truth, whether to spend money or save it, whether to get married, and to whom, and thousands of other things. Many of these decisions are simple and unimportant (e.g., whether I buy a green car or a blue one), but others can have deep and far reaching implications in our lives, such as a choice to get married, have children, or build a business on unfair on illegal practices. All of these decisions are "moral" because they are choices about values, i.e., what we want to preserve, about what we ought to do and who we want to be. When we fail to make moral decisions we give up our freedom and allow the course of our life to be determined by something or someone else. None of us wants to do that.

Morality as feeling. There are many different ways in which people make moral choices. Some people rely heavily on their feelings or intuitions to tell them what course of action they should follow. When faced with the possibility of taking property that rightfully belongs to another, for example, someone might experience emotional revulsion and say, "I just don't feel that is the right thing to do." If pressed, they might say, "I don't know why, but it just doesn't feel right." In this case, a moral choice would arise primarily from an emotional reaction, and would be like saying, "Theft really makes me angry." Similarly, we might rely on a kind of moral intuition, or little voice, which tells us what is right and wrong. Like "feminine intuition," moral intuition "just knows" moral truth. That knowledge can be accurate and penetrating. But it also is hard to explain to others. Someone who makes moral decisions on the basis of an intuition may be absolutely convinced of the rightness or wrongness of the choice, but cannot explain it to anyone else because intuitions and emotions are essentially private and individual. When we decide by saying "I feel," we are in our own world of moral opinion. Authentic moral decision making, on the other hand, must be more than a private feeling and must involve discussion and dialogue with others.

Morality as duty. There are other ways of making moral decisions, those based on rules against which we compare our behavior to determine its moral correctness. These approaches formulate rules by asking one of two questions: "What is my duty?" or "What will make me happy?"

The first approach to morality begins with the authority of a lawmaker to establish law and our duty to obey it. In this approach the main virtue is obedience to the will of the lawmaker, at least as far as this can be determined, and it does not encourage discussion or questioning. It is not unlike the mother who tells her child to do something and the child asks, "But why?" Many mothers know that explanations are usually not the beginning of fuller obedience, so they simply say, "Because I said so, that's why." In this case, mother is placing a duty to obey her upon the child. She is asserting her authority as the one who knows what is good for the child, and her rules require obedience. She knows in many cases it is better to rely on authority than to get into a lengthy discussion of why she demands this particular course of action from the child.

Decision making based on duty can take many shapes. Some approaches have tried to use reason to arrive at moral norms which are absolute and universal and which apply to everyone without exception. One such norm might be "Do nothing which you would not want everyone else to be able to do, as well." On that basis, for example, we could rule out lying or theft, since none of us would want to be lied to or burglarized. Here the "authority" is reason itself, which has construed these absolute rules for human behavior.

Another kind of duty-based morality more familiar to us today is biblical where the authority is the word of God. Here the will of God is known to us through Scripture and our duty is to obey it. This method is largely characteristic of religious fundamentalism where moral truth is sought exclusively in "the book" and imposes an absolute duty to obey. Some see even questioning these Scriptural norms as the beginning of disobedience. The problem, as we will discuss later, is that Scripture does not treat every moral question we face today, and we have always made some scriptural norms (e.g., the prohibition of killing) more binding than others (e.g., turning the other cheek). This in itself is a process of interpretation which prioritizes the Scriptural word and makes some passages more binding than others.

Morality as the search for happiness. Catholic morality is often caricatured as authoritarian, ("Do what Father says") but in fact it is not. Rather than making obedience and duty the primary components of morality, the heart of Catholic morality is in the notion of *happiness*, which is, as St. Augustine and St. Thomas Aquinas agree, the purpose of human life, or the reason for which we exist. God created us to be happy, and has planted this desire for happiness deep within us. So morality is not a merely a matter of obedience to some external authority, but rather the search for real, enduring satisfaction in life. For this reason, Catholic morality is *goal-based* rather than *duty-based*, and the goal God asks us to seek is happiness and human fulfillment. The Baltimore Catechism used to ask, "Why did God create me?" and we answered, "To know him, love him, serve him in this world and be happy forever with him in the next." That reminds us that God created all of us – even those who do not know God or believe in him – to be with him. When we are truly happy and fulfilled as human persons, we know that we have discovered some of that plan for us, and we have begun to discover what it means to be moral.

This plan is like the operating instructions which accompany a fine piece of equipment. In order to make the equipment function well, there are certain things one must do and certain other things one must not do. One should not, for example, put sand in a coffee maker: it violates the "purpose" of the coffee maker and will probably ruin it. Similarly, the human person is a finely tuned, divinely created organism which has a purpose. Some kinds of behavior are "good for us," or make us happy and well-functioning, while other kinds of behavior are bad for us and impair our performance. The things which contribute to real well-being and long-term happiness are what we call morality. Those which violate us, make us miserable and offend God's good wishes for us are immoral, or sinful. We say, for example that when freely chosen, excessive drinking is morally wrong because humans fall far short of who they can be when they stagger, stammer, get sick and suffer hangovers. Too much (or too little) of anything unbalances us and makes us less than we should be.

So morality is not simply a process of obeying a set of written instructions with no idea of why we should do so, but rather of discovering, over a lifetime, what is truly fulfilling and healthy for us. Parents must sometimes tell children to do something "because I said so." But for adults, morality becomes a process of discovering God's built-in plan for us, learning what really fulfills and brings happiness *in the long run*. This last qualification is important because otherwise we end up absorbed in instant gratification, seeking pleasure only for the moment. Rather than saying, "I will steal this television because there is a program I wish to see this evening," we might say, "I wish to see this program today, and it is a good program which would make me a better person. But in the interest of justice and the security and trust of my neighbors, I will not steal a television to do so." In this process we have taken one good (the admittedly helpful television show) and subordinated it to another, more important good (justice and community security), and have thereby chosen the long-term good over the short-term one.

Catholic morality does not ask us to obey blindly, but to understand how these teachings lead us to fulfillment. This is obviously not child's play. It is an adult skill that is acquired only with some experience and help. I have met many adults who have never moved beyond a fourth grade, authoritarian understanding of morality and who find the equation "morality equals happiness" threatening. They prefer the security of "being told what to do," rather than taking the time and energy to deliberate about what will truly bring them happiness and fulfillment in the long run. Moral education is of great concern to parents today. It may begin with "Do this because I said so," but cannot stop there. At some point, children must be introduced to the notion of real human goods which fulfill them and be taught to discover those goods themselves. They must learn that "virtue is its own reward," that we seek morality not because someone tells us to but because we know it is a good thing.

In our system of morality, there is only one basic question, viz., "will this choice make me truly happy?" Catholic morality starts with what is naturally fulfilling, but it does not stop there. When I teach morality, I often like to talk about "happiness with a small h" and "Happiness with a big H." The happiness refers to those things which fulfill us as human persons – things like justice, temperance, truthfulness, community, fidelity, etc. These are things which all human persons – not just Catholics – need to survive and be happy.

These natural human values prepare us for Happiness – with a big "H"– which we sometimes describe as "heaven," or ultimate union with God. This means that when God calls us to be with him in heaven, he does so not *in spite of* what is good about human existence, but rather *by means of* the real human values we feel and touch and enjoy. This is what St. Thomas Aquinas meant when he said "Grace perfects nature": when we are really "enjoying ourselves," in the sense that we have realized some of what it means to be truly and fully human, we are "on the track" toward heaven.

When we are fully human – fully truthful, fully faithful, fully healthy and fully just, when our human nature is all it can possibly be, we are open to grace. Grace enters in and completes God's creative act not by altering or changing the goodness of human values, but by perfecting them or "raising the voltage" on them, enabling us one day to actually see God face to face. Someone once remarked, speaking of Roman Catholicism: "Wherever the Roman sun does shine, there's plenty of laughter and good red wine." Practically, this means that Catholics do not see holiness and happiness as incompatible. We don't feel that when "anything that feels good must be a sin."

Catholics are often uncomfortable about sudden, radical religious conversions which change personalities. Although such conversions do take place, the Catholic understanding of grace makes them unlikely: we believe that God prefers to "work through" us, gradually enhancing what is naturally good about us by grace, rather than radically destroying us and replacing us by grace. This is why the church has repeatedly denounced heresies which deny the goodness of human nature. Human nature, far from being the "root of all evil," is good basic material which is not obliterated by grace but made better and perfected by it. Human enjoyment is not grace's enemy, but its foundation.

Chapter 3 – Sources of Moral Wisdom: Experience, Reason and Scripture

Finding Happiness Through Experience and Reason

We have shown how Catholic morality, at its root, is a search for happiness and human fulfillment. But how do we go about finding it? Our tradition offers us three rich sources: human experience, reason, and Scripture.

I was once explaining to my mother, who is not Catholic, what a moral theologian did for a living. I told her I tried to teach people how to think about moral issues, use the Bible in morality and arrive at good moral decisions in medical ethics, sexual morality and public policy. "Goodness," she said, "I don't know how you would teach people all those things. You just know what to do and then do it."

My mother's response was an accurate picture of Protestant ethics, which tends to rely heavily on the Bible and on one's personal reflection on God's will in our lives. Catholic morality, on the other hand, is systematic, often looks like a law book, and is not always directly derived from Scripture. It has a long and sometimes mysterious history and can be baffling to those who do not understand its roots.

The term "moral" means simply "what we ought to do," and we make moral decisions in many different ways. Sometimes we rely on our emotions or on a "sixth sense" to "feel" the right course of action. Other times, like many in the Protestant tradition, we look to the Bible for moral answers. Still other times we avoid religion or theology at all, preferring to use reasonable reflection about human experience to come to sound ethical conclusions. The Catholic moral tradition uses all three – emotions, the Word of God, and reason – to shape its approach to moral decision making. But if one thing characterizes the Catholic approach, it is our reliance on reason and common sense to arrive at "what we ought to do." We believe that any person of good will, even a non-Christian, can live a morally good life by careful reflection on moral choices.

The reason for this lies in the Catholic belief that grace (i.e., God's creative power) is present in our very natures. Even though Catholics are sometimes seen as being obsessed with sin, our theological tradition is a very optimistic one. We do not believe that the human person is depraved, perverse or naturally sinful. Rather, we believe that God created us good, and that we participate in God's own life. This makes us essentially good, though certainly our freedom and the reality of original sin make the struggle for holiness a difficult one.

So while Catholics have at times found a certain fascination with "sins," in the last analysis we believe that grace has already made us good, and we do not get bogged down in the notion of "sin" as a condition which totally corrupts the human person. This belief is at the root of our practice of frequent confession: it is not a way of emphasizing how sinful we are at our core, but a way of describing that we are restored to our natural goodness when sins are healed by God's renewing grace.

This fundamental optimism about the person has important implications for the way we make moral decisions. If we truly thought human beings were depraved and fundamentally flawed by sin, we could not trust the human mind to work well enough to know moral goodness and make sound decisions. Such a view would lead us to depend entirely on the Scriptural word of God – rather than upon God's grace in our lives. It would also make the moral life a series of individual, disconnected choices, but would not necessarily help us be "good persons" who would gradually develop virtues and moral skills. Catholics tend to favor the view that grace is present in us in such a way that to some extent we can "trust" our minds and hearts to know moral good and choose it. This means that we can, to some extent, trust our human experience to tell us what is morally good and bad. Through careful reflection, we can discover that those things which we experience as pleasant, fulfilling and wholesome as "good," and those things which are painful, limiting and frustrating as "bad."

St. Thomas Aquinas says that human persons are not created just *in* the image of God, as static images in a mirror, but "*into* the image of God" – in the sense of a dynamic movement toward fuller union with God. This means that by grace we grow to be more and more like God, actually knowing some of God's plan for us. And although some of this plan is revealed to us in Scripture many of the details, especially in moral matters, are discoverable by reason or common sense – the one ability humans alone possess which has always been understood as making us closest to God. Our reason, though certainly able to make mistakes and choose selfishly, is a "spark of divinity" which can be trusted, with the help of grace, to see reality clearly enough to make good moral decisions. This is an astounding fact which gives us as humans a tremendous dignity and responsibility. In giving us the gift of reason, God has given us a truly graced freedom. We are not entirely reliant on external directions, but have built in "moral compasses" which, when properly trained, can help us discover holiness and true human happiness.

Natural Law: Knowing by Being

While Scripture obviously plays an important part in moral decision making, I would like to focus briefly on our reasonable moral decision-making ability. Theologians call this natural law.

Natural law is frequently misunderstood and even abused, but it is the heart of the moral tradition in Catholicism. Let me highlight a few important facts about natural law and the role in plays in morality.

First of all, natural law is only "law" in a certain sense. In general, law can be described as "a reasonable rule enacted for the common good." Within that general definition, there are different levels of law. The eternal law, for example, is the plan for all creation that is in the mind of God, much like the plan for a new building is in the mind of an architect. Divine law articulates parts of that plan; the prescription to love one's neighbor would be a good example. Natural law is one step lower, and contains those parts of God's plan which may not be found explicitly in Scriptures, but which are discovered through discussion, research and dialogue. Natural law itself has levels, too, from the most general, like "do good and avoid evil," to more and more detailed rules which require more thought, such as "honor the elderly," "charge reasonable interest on loans," and "control the possession of dangerous weapons." These moral rules are all based on reason, but the more detailed they become, the more controversy they engender. Current disputes about gun control laws certainly prove that.

Civil laws are those with which we are most familiar and include state, civil and federal laws which are enacted by legislatures or courts. These laws, if they are good ones, clearly reflect the general definition above: they are reasonable, clearly known to the public which they bind, and directed to the good of all rather than to merely private goods. This is why we see politicians who enact laws which favor their own narrow interests as undesirable. These laws, while related to natural law because they are reasonable, are much more specific than natural law and much less flexible.

The second important fact about natural law is that it is *based on human nature*. (It is important to note that natural law is not the same as the *laws of nature*, which are animal instincts and physical laws which determine the boiling temperature of water and the amount of wing surface and thrust necessary to safely lift a jet off the ground.) Natural law is unique to humans because it is a process of reasonable thought which only humans can do. It looks at human nature and tries to determine what is good for humans, that is, what is moral. In this sense, we "know by being". As we understand who we are we are able to formulate some rules for what will make us truly happy.

"Nature" as it is understood here is a complex and sometimes elusive reality. Discovering what "human nature" is requires the expertise of the biological and physical sciences, psychology, spirituality, and philosophy. Since the human person is mysterious, we never fully discover what it means to be a person. Our understanding is always evolving. This is why there is a historical dimension to human nature. Human persons are products of culture and history, and when asking "What is human nature," we must also ask, "How has human nature been shaped by the forces of history and culture?" Are twentieth century Americans, for example, essentially the same as a person living in China in 5000 BC? There are certainly some things which remain constant about human nature, but changes and developments occur, as well, so we must constantly redefine what we mean by "person" in order to determine what kinds of behavior best fulfills that person.

Nature also has a social dimension to it, since human beings do not exist in the abstract but only in community. So when we ask what is "natural," we must take account of the community in which we live. Morality is not only about what is good for *me*, as a solitary individual, but for me as a member of society. My good and my moral choices are linked to the good of those around me. This social dimension of natural law reminds us that it touches all areas of morality and not just biology or sex, with which it is commonly linked.

One of the most important things about our natural law tradition is that it enables us to talk about ethical matters with people who do not share our religious beliefs. This is why the American Bishops, for example, were able to write pastoral letters on nuclear war and the economy which generated considerable interest from the rest of society. The White House, in fact, wrote a letter to the Bishops as they were formulating their pastoral letter on nuclear arms, questioning their teaching on the deterrent value of nuclear arms. The statements made in the Bishops' letters were not based solely on Scripture (which would have rendered them largely irrelevant to non-believers) but on reason-able arguments rooted in common human values which other members of a pluralistic society – including White House policy makers – could understand and debate. The just war theory, which tries to limit both the justification and extent of warfare, was developed largely by Roman Catholic theologians. It has been an important part of political theory for centuries because it was written in natural law terms which made it understandable to nations all over the world.

Catholicism's natural law tradition puts the church in a unique position in society. While we can speak confidently about morality from a religious perspective, we are also able to speak about it in human terms which are understandable to others who do not share our religious beliefs. What is more, we can do so knowing that when we discover something that is truly fulfilling on a human level, we have at least the foundation for grace and supernatural fulfillment. We are thus able to stand with one foot in society at large, and one foot in our own church community. This is why Catholic thinkers have played such a significant role in determining public policy (e.g., John A. Ryan, a Catholic theologian who was instrumental in developing the concept of minimum wage, or Msgr. George Higgins, who wrote widely on labor relations in our own time).

Some Catholics today would like us to retreat into a smaller church, one which would "mind its own business" and avoid involvement in political and social issues. Fortunately, our own common sense moral tradition, based on natural law, human fulfillment and reason, will not easily allow us to do that. Because we believe that society and nature are suffused with grace, and that reason enables all people of good will to discover that grace in human fulfillment, we are bound to discover what we can of God's plan for us even in a pluralistic society.

The Bible as a Source of Moral Wisdom

As the revealed word of God, the Bible holds a place of privilege in Christian ethics. Along with experience and reason, it provides us with a third source of moral wisdom. Yet there are different ways of using Scripture to arrive at moral decisions, some more fruitful than others. Let us look at several possibilities.

I have seen a bumper sticker that reads: "God said it, I believe it, that settles it." That bumper sticker reflects a fundamentalistic approach to Scripture. It implies that God has all the answers and makes them directly available to us in Scripture. It implies that all we needed to do was consult the Bible and we would be able to find the answers to any moral problem that faced us. It suggests that Scripture alone could be our moral guide, without recourse to any other sources of moral wisdom, and perhaps even that God does not reveal moral wisdom any place other than in the pages of Scripture.

Catholics would find this understanding of the Bible unfamiliar, especially in moral matters. Unlike our Protestant brothers and sisters, we were not accustomed to frequent contact with the Bible. While we certainly hold the Bible in esteem, Catholics have historically tended to prefer the dramatic and ritual enactment of the mysteries of salvation through our sacraments, art and liturgy rather than only through the spoken or written word. Similarly, our moral tradition is based not primarily upon Scripture, but upon reflection about what is truly fulfilling to human nature. For us, morality is what makes us truly and fully happy in the long run, a fact which is largely verifiable by our experience. If that is so, then we might legitimately ask what the role of Scripture is in moral decision making. Is it merely icing on the cake, or does it serve as an important source for wisdom for us?

Various Uses of Scripture in Morality

The bumper sticker I used to see reflects one way in which we might use the Bible as a source of moral wisdom. Another is *proof-texting*, a cut and paste exercise in which we arrive at a decision on a particular issue and then seek supporting evidence for it from Scripture. This is relatively easy since the Bible is large and has ambiguous or conflicting statements which can be used to support many different moral choices. Nazi Germans appealed to Scripture to support their genocide, 19th century Americans used it to uphold slavery, and many today claim to find support for position on gun control or gay marriage.

At the opposite extreme are those who deny any relevance at all to the Scriptural witness. They feel that since the words of Scripture were written so long ago, for unknown audiences, they cannot possibly have anything to say to us. Unlike those who see perfect agreement between Scriptural times and our own age, these people feel that historical changes that have taken place since the Bible was written are so drama-tic that they render the Bible useless to us in modern times.

A final approach, which most closely characterizes the Catholic understanding, is that Scripture has priority as one important source of moral wisdom, but that by itself it is inadequate to provide moral norms. This is true for a number of reasons, namely, that the Bible, as a source of moral wisdom is in incomplete, not fully in agreement and must be interpreted.

Incompleteness. Although the Biblical witness is lengthy and complex, there are many contemporary moral issues which it does not treat. The question of *in vitro* fertilization, for example, has no scriptural treat-ment at all and could not have been envisioned by the pre-technical mindset of biblical writers. Similarly, questions of organ trans-plantation or withdrawing hydration and nutrition from seriously ill patients finds no resolution in Scripture. And even though the Bible has something to say about war, in no way could it have anticipated the advent of chemical or nuclear weapons which clearly present a new moral situation.

Lack of Unity. In other cases, Scripture addresses problem or moral question, but with conflicting evidence. Many passages in the Old Testament, for example, seem to extol the glory of war as a sign of

God's protective favor to the Israelites. In the New Testament, Jesus himself says that he has "come to bring a sword, not peace," (Mt 10:34); elsewhere he reminds the disciples that they might need their swords (Lk 22:36). Yet other passages seem starkly to contradict these. In Matthew 26:52, Jesus says that those "who live by the sword will die by the sword," (Mt 26:52); and more than once he urges people to do good to those who persecute them, or to "turn the other cheek and offer no resistance." Over the centuries both the just war theory (which allowed the use of violence if certain criteria were met) and pacifism (which eschewed all violence as inappropriate to Christians) found support in these Scriptural passages. Today, both are legitimate options for Christians.

In the matter of wealth and poverty, Jesus says in one place that his disciples should "sell all they have," and that it is "more difficult for a rich man to enter the kingdom of heaven than for a camel to pass through the eye of a needle." Yet elsewhere he uses the parable of the talents to suggest that we should be wise in our investments.

Interpretation. Even when Scripture does treat of a particular moral, issue, and does so without apparent contradiction, there is still the problem of understanding what the writer meant. Some passages, like the Ten Commandments, are relatively clear and easy to understand, but they are also very general. It is also important to remember that at least the last seven commandments (honor they father and mother, do not steal, do not lie, etc.) are also part of the natural law; that is, they reflect basic human values which can be discovered by reason without the help of revelation. Any reasonable person, even one without religious faith, can understand that killing, lying and adultery are wrong.

Other passages are more troublesome. In one crucial passage relating to the permissibility of divorce, for example, Matthew says that divorce is permissible only in some cases:

> Whoever divorces his wife – lewd conduct is a separate case – and marries another commits adultery, and the man who marries a divorced woman commits adultery... [Mt 19:9]

But it is not clear whether one word, translated here as "lewd conduct" means unchastity, incest, or adultery. The problem is further complicated by the fact that in his gospel Mark quotes Jesus as saying "Whoever divorces his wife and marries another commits adultery against her" [Mk 10:11], and does not mention the exception found in Matthew. To this day, Catholics have held that divorce is never permissible, and that Matthew's exception refers only to the permissibility of separation without remarriage and not to divorce as such. Over the centuries the church has chosen to *interpret* the vague and conflicting scriptural evidence in this way, because the scriptural answer itself is not crystal clear.

How is the Bible Useful for Morality?

Given these problems of history and interpretation, is the Bible useless to us in answering moral questions? Far from it, if we understand the purpose of the Bible. It is important to remember that there are a number of levels of moral teaching ranging from very specific moral laws to more general attitudes, values and goals. While the Bible responds to all of them, it is more useful at some levels than at others. A number of writers including James Gustafson, William Spohn and Lisa Cahill have described these levels in various ways. One way of summarizing them would be as follows.

Laws and specific decisions. Morality has largely to do with specific decisions in particular situations, and many times these decisions are guided by laws which tell us what to do. The Bible does contain specific moral laws (such as those found in Leviticus 14 which describes how the priest is to offer sacrifice and purify lepers), but as we have already shown, there are many other important moral questions which are not covered at all. So we might say that the Bible has some relevance at the level of specific laws and decisions, but it is not a reference book in which we can find all the answers. An example is found in Paul's letter to the Romans, where Paul addresses a particular church community and refers to dietary requirements which are no longer binding for us:

> Extend a kind welcome to those who are weak in faith. Do not enter into disputes with them. A man of sound faith knows he can eat anything, while one who is weak in faith eats only vegetables... [14:1-2]

Paul alludes here to a very specific moral law, but it is so specific to the time and culture of the first century church that it seems irrelevant to us.

Moral norms are more general than moral laws and could be addressed to any believing community. Again, from Paul as he speaks to the Romans:

> Owe no debt to anyone except the debt that binds us to love one another. He who loves his neighbor has fulfilled the law. [13:8]

At this level, the scriptural word is general but it yields more information than it would if we were looking for specific moral laws relating to specific situations.

Values, goals and ideals are the concrete goods-to-be-sought. They are the basis for both moral laws and moral norms, and without them moral laws would be completely arbitrary. They provide the "why" for moral teachings. Unity, friendship, community togetherness and care for one another are all reasons why Paul exhorts the Romans to love and tolerate of those who are weak in faith. Although eating meat sacrificed to idols is no longer an issue for us today, we still seek the values and ideals of church community which Paul held so dear and tried to demonstrate to the early church.

The Bible and Christian Character. The scriptural writers were interested in laws, norms and ideals. But they were even more interested *in forming a people.* Their message, which contained God's own call to be the people of God, was spoken to shape the Jews, and later Christians, into the chosen people who would be exhibit certain kinds of characteristics. So while Scripture is sometimes helpful in telling us what *kinds of choices* we should make, it is far more helpful in teaching us *what kinds of persons* we should be.

In the Catholic tradition, answers to specific questions are usually reasoned out from available knowledge about human nature and community. We do not look to the Bible for answers about genetic engineering, for example; rather, we ask "What does it mean to be human?" and from that we deduce God's purpose in creating us and try to discover the extent to which we might alter our genetic makeup. Instead of providing concrete answers to detailed scientific questions such as these, the Bible forms our attitudes, values and character – shaping us into disciples – persons who think clearly and lovingly about the moral questions that we face. Scripture does not contradict human moral wisdom, but illuminates the norms we arrive at through reason, making them clearer and more appealing.

Christians should allow themselves to be bathed in the word of Scripture. Looking to Scripture for specific answers is not bad, but it can be frustrating and at odds with the reasons for which the evangelists or prophets originally wrote. Through its liturgy, the Church provides exposure to a significant portion of the Scriptural word. The weekday readings we hear at Mass on Sundays and week-days give us long segments of the four evangelists, St. Paul, and the Hebrew Scriptures. The point is not to give us a moral text book, but to relate the Christian story from many different perspectives so that our understanding of it becomes fuller and fuller over the years. Gradually, our moral sense is trained by these words, so that we come to choose well naturally and easily.

Theologians who study Scripture for its moral message know that it is important to see Scripture as a whole, to respect the kind of writing any particular passage represents, and to take careful account of the historical and cultural setting in which the passage was written. The poetry of the psalms, for example, must be understood in a different light than the admonitions of St. Paul to his early Church communities, which were written centuries later and for different reasons.

Preaching and the Moral Life

St. Paul asked the Romans, "How will they hear unless someone preaches?" Preaching makes the biblical word come to life. It is the church's way of leading us into a fuller experience of grace. Unfortunately, preaching on morality has gotten a bad name because of "fire and brimstone" preaching which scolds and berates people. Good preaching helps us see our sins, but it should also see our lives in a different light, lead us to do something concrete as a result of our faith, and show us how to find the happiness which is the heart of morality. Good preachers use the Scriptural word not only to show us where we have fallen short, but to illuminate grace in our lives and make us thirst for a greater portion of it.

Preaching is not just a lecture. It can be described as a *persuasive conversation* which involves the preacher, the Word of God, and the congregation. It requires that the preacher understand the scriptural word, preach from faith and humility, and use rhetorical and communication skills which move us to action. Preaching should move us to reform our personal lives, and it should bring the church as a whole into deeper dialogue with society on important social issues.

Because of our love for the liturgy, art and music of the church, Catholics sometimes neglect the importance of preaching. In addition to studying the word of Scripture ourselves, we should also expect our priests to preach conscientiously on the biblical texts, relating them carefully to the moral issues we face in our daily lives. Preachers must look first to the moral issues that surround them (the morning paper is a good place to start) and then ask, "What do today's Scripture readings have to say to this issue?" After teaching a course entitled "Preaching on Moral Issues" for several years, I am convinced that any set of readings can yield an effective word on any moral issue that faces us.

Yves Congar, the great theologian of Vatican II who was made a cardinal by Pope John Paul II in 1994 once said that if there were two countries, one which had only preaching, and the other which had only the Eucharist, faith would be stronger in that country with only preaching. This suggests how important preaching is to the spiritual, moral and liturgical life of the church. Priests and others who preach must take their responsibility much more seriously, and allow sufficient time for study, prayer and reflection on the biblical word.

The responsibility for preaching is shared by those in the pews, too. They must let the preacher know that they listen to what he or she says, and they must be active participants in the act of preaching. No preacher can carry the burden of making God's word come alive all by himself. Those of us who hear preaching must listen attentively, offer critique and comment, and make the dialogue that goes on between priest and church a strong and vital one.

PART II: THE HEART OF CATHOLIC MORALITY

Chapter 4 – Conscience as Our Moral Compass

We have explored how experience, reason and Scripture all serve us as we approach specific moral decisions. Conscience uses them all. Conscience is the human capacity, at once a kind of "moral vision" or "compass" and a judgment, which enables us to relate all three of them to the particular problem that faces us.

The United States Government has what is sometimes referred to as its "Conscience Fund." Over the years, people, usually anonymously, send checks to this fund to make good on unpaid taxes, thefts, or other injustices which are sometimes never even specified. The fund receives hundreds of thousands of dollars a year, and each receipt signals that someone has rethought the moral implications of something they had done in the past. One might say that people returning the money had "guilty consciences," or that their "consciences were bothering them."

This reflects one common understanding of conscience: it is a "feeling" which won't leave us alone, which tries to tell us that we have either done something wrong, or have failed to do something we should have done.

Another way we often understand conscience is something that is in opposition to the law. Someone who deliberately violates the law, for example, is sometimes called a "conscientious objector." We occasionally read of highly conscientious people who deliberately set out to be arrested by trespassing on private property to protest abortion, cross government lines to stage a "sit-in" at a plant which builds destructive weapons, or refuse to report for duty when drafted for military service. These cases suggest that sometimes conscience is at odds with the law or custom, and that we must either follow the law or follow our consciences.

Conscience as a "Warehouse of Values"

The reality of conscience is at once more complex and more simple than this. At one level, conscience is our basic awareness of good and evil. Each of us can probably recall a moment early in our lives when we first realized that some things are to be done merely because they are "right," while others are to be avoided because they are "wrong." Very young children do not have this ability – they do what they are told because "mommy said so," or because they fear getting caught and punished. With the help of experience and parental guidance, however, children gradually move to the point of their "first moral act" – the first time they act not out of fear of punishment or obedience, but because they realize that stealing, lying or cruelty are wrong and harmful. Whenever that moment comes (and most of us probably don't recall exactly when it was) we have the first spark of conscience. We have the first brick of what author Vincent Rush has called our "warehouse of values," the place where we "store" our moral knowledge, awareness and sensitivity, to be drawn on all through the rest of our lives.[3]

Parents see this in their children, and might be thrilled by the first time a child comes home from school and announces that even though she had stolen a toy from a playmate, she had come to realize that it was bad to do that and had returned the toy. Rudimentary as it seems, this is the first time the child understands what "good" and "evil" are, and the first time the child has made an authentic moral choice.

Some peoples' "warehouses" of values are vast and well-stocked, while other people never seem to develop one at all. Others develop values and goals, but they seem warped and disoriented. The movie "Silence of the Lambs," for example, focused on a psychopathic killer named Hannibal Lecter who was highly intelligent; yet because of mental illness, he had no apparent awareness of the moral value of human life. Though imprisoned, he escaped and repeatedly performed vicious acts of mutilation and murder. These acts horrify us, and are clearly the product of a sick mind; but they are also extreme examples of a lack of moral values which shape the decisions we make.

Conscience is more than just moral awareness, or a place where we keep our moral values. It is also practical, that is, it must come to bear on practical decisions-about-what-is-to-be-done-here-and-now. It is not just something hidden away in the recesses of our minds, but something which must shape our decisions and our lives. We must make practical, specific decisions about many different things: Whether to repay a loan or take office supplies from the company for which we work; whether to engage in sex with someone to whom we are not married; whether to try to achieve conception by some means of *in vitro* fertilization; whether to continue medical treatments "at all costs," or to forego some, even though it might mean our lives (or those for whom we are making decisions) are shortened.

Conscience as an Ability to Choose

In these concrete instances, conscience takes on a different character. It is no longer just a set of values and goals, or a vague "feeling" which prompts us to "feel guilty" about something we have done or might do, but rather a hard-nosed, careful *judgment* about what we must do. Should I cheat on my taxes and use the money to may my child's tuition? Should I miss Mass in favor of visiting a sick friend? Should I give to this charity or that, or to none at all? Should I persevere in a difficult and abusive marriage, or abandon it for my own health and perhaps the good of my children? Should I undergo this difficult and painful medical treatment, with some small hope that it will make me better, or should I use my remaining days to prepare myself spiritually?

Decisions of conscience like this are not easy, because they rarely present us with two stark alternatives, one good and one evil. Almost inevitably, we are presented with two goods: the good of money for tuition versus the good of civic duty to pay taxes; the good of spiritual benefit of mass versus the need of a sick friend; the good of fidelity in marriage versus my (or my children's) psychological and spiritual welfare; the good of sexual pleasure versus the good of faithfulness, wholeness and honesty. So rather than having merely good and evil to choose from, conscience, as a judgment, must choose carefully among many different goods and often find a balance among them. For this reason, the exercise of conscience is really a skill which we acquire over a lifetime. Far from being just a feeling which arises involuntarily from within us, conscience is a highly developed awareness of moral good and evil as well as an act of judgment about how that moral good is to be realized in this particular instance.

Conscience is complex, but it can be described in three basic steps: deliberation, decision and action.

Deliberation: Deliberation is primarily a matter of *gathering information and establishing options* about the choice before us. It is the most detailed of the three steps, and has several parts. The first step of deliberation is *seeing reality as it is,* since, like a captain piloting a ship in the fog, we cannot make good decisions about things we cannot see. I am reminded of the story of a priest who was about to have surgery to remove his appendix. After his surgeon carefully explained the procedure to him, he asked him if he understood the procedure. The priest assured the surgeon he did, but had one question: "Will the scar show above my collar?" Obviously, the priest didn't see the reality of the surgery very well, and was not prepared to make a good decision about it. A judgment of conscience begins with a clear understanding of the question we face.

A second dimension of deliberation is *consultation*, or seeking the opinion and expertise of those around us. We do this not only because other people may have wisdom we do not possess (especially in technical matters, such as those relating to health care) but also because our decisions have social implications which affect other people. We sometimes think of morality as a "private matter" which does not concern others, but it is a rare moral choice which has absolutely no implications for someone else. Even choices relating to sexual conduct, which we usually consider to be personal, can have vast social consequences if the choice results in destabilizing a marriage or spreading a sexually transmitted disease.

Consulting others can also be a helpful way of avoiding excessive self-interest or prejudice which affects our judgment. Even when we try to be objective, our self-interest and subjectivity can get in the way of a good decision. I am reminded of a man who came to see me about a relationship he was having with a woman who worked in his office. Although the relationship had grown to involve sexual intimacy, he had prevented himself from seeing that and was shocked when I used the word "adultery." "It isn't *adultery,*" he said with a hurt look on his face. But as we discussed it, his vision became clearer and he admitted he didn't want to want to see it as adultery because the relationship had been so rewarding for him. Just as we ask a lawyer's advice before deciding whether to file a lawsuit, so in many moral decisions we should consult those whose opinions and moral maturity and objectivity we respect.

Another dimension of deliberation is *memory*. When we face moral decisions, there are often events in our own past which can put a helpful light on the situation at hand. As we deliberate, we should always search our own past experience to see if there is anything similar which has happened in the past, and if so, what alternatives, consequences and possibilities existed at the time. Although our ability to do this is limited when we are young (which is why we sometimes say that experience is the best teacher), as we grow older our cumulative memory grows too, and we have more and more wisdom and experience upon which to draw.

"Remembering" also involves church tradition and teaching, since this is the body of accumulated wisdom passed on from one age to another. This is why church teaching plays such an important role in decisions of conscience. Sometimes we hear people say, "I had to decide whether to follow the church's teaching or follow my conscience" – but this is a false dichotomy. It is rarely a question of having to choose one over another, but of allowing conscience to *use* church teaching as it uses other kinds of memory to inform choice. Church teaching on a particular matter may not always provide us with an exact answer to a specific question, but it tells us far more than we can know on our own as individuals because it contains reaches back through centuries of Christian experience. Church tradition in moral matters functions like a road sign: it points us in a direction and helps us get where we are going. There may be detours or exceptional cases along the way, but generally the church's wisdom should weigh heavily in the moral decisions we make. We should depart from it regretfully and only after prayerful deliberation.

Deciding. When we have finished the process of deliberation, we must eventually decide – that is, come to a determination about how to achieve the best possible balance of good in this particular case. After we have looked carefully at the case before us, taken counsel, remembered both our own experience and that of the church, we must decide what to do, since in the last analysis conscience is a practical function – it always leads to a decision.

Emotions are important here, too. Sometimes emotions can be detrimental to good decision making, for instance if we are so angry that we "can't see straight." But emotions always play some role in deciding and we must listen to them. If we "feel," for example that a proposed course of action is wrong, we must take that into account because sometimes our emotions "know" moral goodness or evil before we apprehend it with our minds. As human persons we have feelings as well as reason and will, and all three of these must come into play as we decide. And when we make a moral decision that is felt, and reasoned and willed all at once, we use all our human ability and make a fully human decision.

Although it may seem obvious, *action* is the final stage of conscience. Once we have deliberated and decided what ought to be done, we must do it. When we fail to do so, we sin, for we know what is to be done, yet we fail to act.

Taken together, these steps represent what we mean by "formation of conscience." Our conscience is one of our human abilities, and we train it just as we train our brains or our muscles. A "bad conscience" or a "lazy conscience" is one that has been trained poorly: it does not have an adequate store of values, it does not know how to deliberate, or it can't come to a decision, or it lacks the courage to act. Whenever these defects are voluntary, they involve sin, because they reflect an unwillingness "to do the right thing."

Our conscience is our moral vision. It is the only way we can see the moral reality before us the only way we can choose. This is why courts sometimes hold hearings to determine whether a person accused of a crime is "competent to stand trial." What the court really wants to know is whether this person understands good and evil and has the ability to choose. In short, the court is asking, "Does this person's conscience function well enough to bear responsibility for a crime?"

Because our conscience is the only way we can see morally, we are bound to follow our judgment of conscience even when it is in error. If I deliberate, decide and act on a particular course of action with sincerity and good intention, I am bound by that choice. I must act on it. This is why some persons, during war, reach the conclusion that war is immoral and refuse to fight, despite public pressure, legal censures and even prison terms. So even when our decisions are at odds with church teaching, if they are _fully conscientious and sincere_, we must follow them. When we depart from church tradition, from counsel given by others, from our own past experience we are getting further and further out on a limb. But if, we take the steps of choice as carefully as we can, appropriating the moral values before us as fully as we know how, we can trust our conscience as a faithful friend who will help us see – and choose – clearly and dependably.

Chapter 5 – Fundamental Choices
for Good and Evil

The movie *The Age of Innocence* is a lush portrayal of Edith Wharton's novel of the same name. It is the story of a young man and woman set against the background of high society and its rigid mores and class structure in late 19th century New York. It focuses on a young man played by Jeremy Irons and an expatriate divorcee played by Michelle Pfeiffer. In the course of the movie, their deep love for one another blossoms passionately but only in the subtle gestures allowed by the times. Both of them are bound: she by her marginal status as a divorcée, he by his betrothal to another woman whom he does not truly love, but who has the proper social status. The movie is an intense, passionate study of moral character which highlights the importance of choice. To the very end of the movie, one is not sure which choice the couple will make: will they indulge their love for one another and shatter previous commitments, or will they choose to forego their mutual satisfaction and remain apart?

Though set in a time whose strictures and formalities seem foreign to us, *The Age of Innocence* reminds us of how crucial choices are to our lives, and how often choices must be made again and again to retain their validity. It also shows how our ability to choose well is limited – or enhanced – by external forces.

Although it seems an unlikely and incongruous sequel, Pope John Paul II's 1993 encyclical, *The Splendor of Truth,* is about choice as well. In the opening paragraphs of his letter, the Pope notes that choice is way of responding to God and the meaning of life itself. The call to make those choices, that is, the call to morality, "deeply touches every person," even those who do not have religious faith. None of us can live a human life and not ask ourselves "Why?" and then "What ought

I to do?" The answer to these questions may be found in religious or non-religious terms, but we can only avoid them by living a completely irresponsible life.

The "Problem" of Freedom

God created us free. We have the ability to know good and evil, and we may choose evil (often under the guise of a very short-term good) if we so desire. Although this freedom is one of the most distinctive marks of what it means to be human, it is also problematic.

Columnist William Pfaff notes that Americans embrace a kind of radically individual freedom, a freedom from restraints, a freedom which allows us to do whatever we want from one moment to the next.[4] On the left, he says, this is characterized by radical personal choice (e.g., to organize protests, have abortions, or refuse military service), on the right by economic individualism and market freedom (e.g., insistence on low taxes, minimal governmental involvement and few social services).

John Paul II maintains that while there is indeed freedom *from* interference and control, there must also be freedom *to*, freedom to make choices and to become certain kinds of persons. The exquisite tension of *The Age of Innocence*, for example, came not only from the free choice which faced the two lovers, that is, whether they would take this or that action here and now, but also the choice-about-who-they-were-to-be. True moral deliberation takes into account not only what we choose to do, but who we choose to be, and the two are intimately related.

One of the primary points of the encyclical addresses this issue. The Pope raises the question of the "fundamental option" and rightly criticizes any understanding of it which separates this "freedom-to-do" from "freedom-to-be." Drawing on the Gospel story of the rich young man, he says that the question the man faces is not just about "rules to be followed, but about the full meaning of life." Although distinct, these two kinds of choices cannot be separated without risking "our substantial integrity and personal unity" (#67). "We create ourselves" by our moral choices (#71); we cannot *do* one thing and *be* another. If I choose to tell a lie, I risk becoming a liar. If I cheat once, I become untrustworthy. The characters in *The Age of Innocence* agonized over whether they could express their love, but even more they worried about what such a choice would do to them as persons.

It is also important to recall, as was so apparent in *The Age of Innocence*, that our free choices are never entirely private and personal. Just as choosing to express their love for one another would have had wide repercussions among those around them, so all of our "free" choices must take others into account. We are radically free, but human freedom, the only kind we know, is also freedom-in-community, whether that be family, city, or world.

What We Know and How We Know It

A second important part of *Veritatis Splendor* revolves around how much we are able to know about morality or human fulfillment. Is there any objective, a once-and-for-all dimension to this "meaning of life?" Are there real, tangible choices that realize it and others that are absolutely at odds with it? Or is my grasp of this meaning as personal and unique as my fingerprint? Is there no way to verify whether I have chosen well?

While the Pope fully acknowledges the importance of subjective factors and circumstances which make my life and my moral choices different from anyone else's, he stresses that there is a "moral order," that is, a way things ought to be, and that there are certain choices which are always at odds with this order, choices which are "intrinsically evil." This is a difficult term. To many, it seems to describe an act which is really, really, disobedient. But at its root, it means an act which by its nature offends who we are as persons. It is not just wrong because someone else says so; it is wrong because it hurts me.

In a commentary on the encyclical, *New York Times* writer Peter Steinfels uses rape as one example of intrinsic evil.[5] Rape is wrong not only "because it offends one's conscience or because society has forbidden it." Rather, it is wrong because it violates the very nature of humanity. It is a fundamental violation of the victim's personhood, and of the perpetrator's human dignity as well. Rape, murder for hire, and fraud true are fundamentally inhuman acts: they are evil in kind, and cannot be justified by any good intention nor mitigated by any circumstances. Even if some very good result were to come of it (e.g., the freedom of a prisoner) we would still say that rape as a means to obtain it is inherently wrong. It has, as Steinfels says, "evil built into its character," so that its moral character is not just "pasted on" but rooted in the act itself. Undertaking an intrinsically evil act, therefore, is far more than being really disobedient. It is a question of doing something fundamentally at odds with what it means to be human.

Although there is debate among theologians as to which acts are intrinsically evil, and how our understanding of them can develop with our understanding of the human person (slavery, for example, was not always seen as intrinsically evil because slaves were not understood as having souls), the encyclical is clear that careful reflection will reveal these abiding truths to us.

How Do We Know?

How do we discover these inherent moral qualities? The second part of the encyclical addresses this question and answers it primarily in terms of natural law. Although this term is often confused with "the laws of nature," which have to do with animal instinct and physics, in fact natural law is a reasonable awareness of the order of creation, of the fact that God created us as one thing and not another, and that this has certain moral implications. If I were to make a vacuum cleaner, for example, which has one purpose, it would certainly have different operating instructions than an iPhone, which has quite a different purpose. This is all the more true for humans, who were created by God as rational, feeling creatures who live in community. Persons have certain operating instruction too, and there are certain acts which are just incompatible with being human, just as there are certain things you cannot do to a vacuum cleaner or a phone. Unlike household appliances, human persons can reflect on who they are and what their purpose is, and that process is called natural law.

The encyclical says that natural law is not just a question of "obedience or rationality" (#64), nor is it only a set of propositions (#88), or mere norms on a biological level (#50). Rather, it is an exercise in reason by which we discover God's eternal plan "implanted in beings endowed with reason and inclining them toward the right action and end" (#44). Not imposed on us like an authoritarian law, natural law is a "participation in God's providence" (#43); as creatures who can think, we are actually able to think like God "thinks," and to some extent, know what God wishes for us.

Far from restrictive or coercive, natural law is an ever-expanding, reasonable awareness of what human life should be. Most importantly, because natural law is a function of reason, it is available to every reasonable person, believer or not. This is why the Pope's encyclical received such widespread attention from the press. It was not speaking only of narrow, religious beliefs, but of the deep, resounding truths of human nature. Not all reasonable persons will immediately agree on what constitutes the fully human, but the importance of the Pope's message is that fundamental agreement is possible, at least on basic moral questions pertaining to life itself, justice and the proper use of our bodies.

The Role of Scripture

The encyclical emphasizes the centrality of reason and natural law, which are the foundation of Catholic morality. The simplicity and universality of this approach in a pluralistic society where many do not share our religious views is obvious. Saying that abortion, lack of housing, or artificial insemination are wrong because they are against the Law of God is persuasive to believers, but not to those who do not believe. Using natural law to show that they are *unreasonable* because they are at odds with what it means to be human will give us a voice even in the most diverse society.

Despite the importance of natural law, the encyclical begins with a long homily on the Gospel story of the rich young man who approaches Jesus and asks him what he must do to be saved. In his long explanation of this passage (which, by the way, is a good model for pastors who might want to preach on moral questions) the Pope uses the rich young man as a symbol for all of us who have the same question. This demonstrates that Scripture is an important source for our moral decisions, too, and that we should use it in conjunction with natural law in shaping our lives. While natural law may provide the rational basis for our choices, Scripture provides the heart, the spirit, and the internal motivation. Just as Jesus gently called the rich young man to follow him as a disciple, so through our personal meditation on Scripture, our Bible study, good preaching, and our participation in liturgy, the same call is extended to us. It does not replace what we know by reason, but fulfills it and brings it to life.

Is This Encyclical for Me?

Recently, as I participated in a symposium on the encyclical, one of the priests in the audience asked, "What are the implications of this for me, as a pastor?" I told him these were the questions moral theologians are afraid someone will ask, because they force us to come down to earth and "make sense of it all." This encyclical may be addressed to the Bishops, yet it is obviously intended as guidance for all of us.

There are at least three central points of abiding importance for all of us.

1) Morality is more than obedience and authority. While the Pope speaks as an authentic moral teacher, he teaches that there is a moral order, a "way-things-ought-to-be" which is built into human nature. It is discovered rather than created, by us. Although the process by which we discover these values is a highly creative participation in God's own mind, it does lead to a definite kind of human fulfillment. We are not adrift on a sea of equally valid choices.

2) The moral life is cumulative, that is, it adds up. Rather than making one-choice-for-all, or a series of choices which have no connection, our moral lives involve many choices that build us up as moral agents and give us character. This is the satisfying part of morality, when we realize that we have begun to "make something of ourselves." Moral wisdom involves learning from our mistakes, doing better next time, and savoring the small victories of commitment, fidelity, compassion, truthfulness, and wholeness which we achieve by grace.

3) The Church has something to say to the world at large. It was amazing how much attention the encyclical received from the secular press. All national newspapers and magazines covered it, and one commentator referred to it as an "Encyclical for Everyman." This shows that the Church, for all its problems, remains a strong and influential voice in the world.

Although this particular document is long and technical, it does provide an incentive to priests to preach more effectively on moral issues (both by opening questions and shaping answers); to scholars and teachers to explore this objective "meaning of life" with students; and to all of us to look carefully for the moral questions that surround us each day. In so doing we will come to see the moral life not as a burden or an oppression, but as an exciting opportunity to shape our future, our society, and ourselves.

Chapter 6 – Whatever Happened to Sin?

In the movie *White Palace*, Susan Sarandon plays a waitress in a hamburger stand in downtown St. Louis. Although she was raised a Catholic, she falls in love with a wealthy Jewish lawyer from the suburbs and the plot of the movie revolves around the disparity of their backgrounds. At one point her friend asks her about her religion. "I used to be Catholic," she said, "but confession made me jumpy."

That's probably a sentiment that could be echoed by a lot of Catholics today. Confession was once an essential identifying characteristic of Catholicism, but it has seen a decline in recent years. This has made many people worry that sin has disappeared. Many parents worry that their children do not value confession as they did, and see this as necessarily a bad sign. But before we answer the question of confession, let's look a little more closely at the reality of sin itself.

The traditional definition of sin was that it was an *act* that involved *serious matter* which was chosen *freely with full knowledge and assent of the will*. More simply put, this meant that in order to commit a sin we had to be free of coercion and pressure, know what we were doing something wrong and still choose to do it. It is important to remember that sin, even though it involves evil, is never a direct choice of evil. No rational person chooses something completely evil. There is always something about the choice that at least *appears* good to them. Sin is more a lack of something which ought to be there than a choice of a positive bad thing. It might be said to be the choice of a good, but of a very limited good.

Sin as disobedience

There are a number of ways in which we can look at sin. One popular way is to understand sin as "breaking the law of God," or "disobeying God" such as when we violate one of the Ten Commandments. Many of us learned a kind of "examination of conscience" which was based on the Ten Commandments: to prepare for confession we asked ourselves whether we had taken the Lord's name in vain, disobeyed our parents, had impure thoughts, etc. While sinful acts do involve breaking the law, this is not an adequate understanding of sin, because it easily lends itself to legalism, that is, saying that "morality" is equal to "obeying the law." The weakness of this is apparent if we think for a moment about the fact that one can obey the letter of the law while ignoring or even abusing its spirit. Someone may, for example, obey the law which prohibits charging excessive interest on a loan while abusing the intent of that law by adding "service charges" to a bill which are really the equivalent of higher interest.

Sin as Relational

We might also understand sin as relational. In this view, we see our relationship or friendship God as weakened or broken. In this case, sin is like offending a good friend. The trust and the joy of the relationship is weakened or destroyed. In more traditional terms, we distinguish between "mortal" and "venial" sins. Mortal sins were those which involved such serious offenses that they killed the relationship with God altogether and we were said to be in a "state of sin," out of communion or friendship with God. Venial sins, on the other hand, were those which weakened the relationship to God but did not entirely destroy it, just as forgetting a luncheon engagement with a friend might cause offense, but would not have the same effect on the friendship as stealing or lying or slander.

This relational view has great appeal to us today because our society is very absorbed in the importance of relationships. In many ways, our society and our view of life are highly psychologized. Our relationships with others – and the things which make them better or worse – are central to our experience. Another advantage of this relational view of sin is that it reminds us that God is a person, and that

45

we may "fall in love" with God just as we fall in love with other humans. Understanding sin as a weakening of that love relationship has many parallels in our own lives, and it helps us see that sin is not just an act against a law, but an act against a person who loves us. In this model, the sacrament of reconciliation does not merely "absolve" us of sin, but helps heal the rift which has occurred because of our offense.

Sin as Choice of a Limited Good

Yet another way of seeing sin is to see it as the choice of a short-term good over a longer term good. This view makes sense if we accept that no rational person chooses pure evil – there is always some apparent good which is the object of choice. The employee who embezzles from her company, for example, does not make a choice for the absolute evil of theft; in her mind, she is choosing the good of economic security for herself or her family, or perhaps the acquisition of certain things which will make life more pleasant. Perhaps she even sees her act as rectifying the injustice of low wages she has received over the years. In another case, a physician may recommend a procedure he knows may not be in the patient's best interest. He does so not to choose evil for the patient, but to choose the short-term good of financial gain, professional prestige (perhaps for perfecting an experimental procedure) or enhancement of his skills. None of these things is evil in itself, but when they are chosen over the greater goods of professional integrity, trust and the commitment of the medical profession to act in the patient's best interest, they can be seen as sin.

We sometimes hear that we should "be all that we can be." Sin is a deliberate choice to be less than we can be: less honest, less caring, less truthful, less whole. Sin in it means choosing for the moment when we know that there are much longer term goods or goals to be sought. Sometimes this is just plain old selfishness; we can't overcome the temptation to choose what is good for *me* rather than what is good for *us*. Other times it is a deliberate unwillingness to discover what the long term goods are.

There are two important things to remember about sin. First, sin is not merely *acting but becoming*. Each time we sin – whether we see it as a disobedient act, an unloving act, or a act which favors a short-term over a long-term good – we affect who we are as persons. The fact that

46

Catholic theology always spoke not only of sins but of a "state of sin," or "vice," reminds us that our acts shape who we are. When we witness a co-worker or friend lie on several occasions, for example, we begin to make a judgment about that person's character or moral identity: we begin to wonder if he is a liar. And to call someone a liar is a much more radical moral judgment than merely to say that someone told a lie. Similarly, while one instance of sexual impropriety does not necessarily a degenerate make, repeated infidelities or promiscuity lead others to judge us as "easy" or worse.

So sin exists on two levels: the level of acts, which can be disobedient, unloving or lacking potential for fulfillment. But sin also exists on the level of character and ultimately shapes who we are as persons. That is why it is important to ask ourselves repeatedly, "Does this act represent the kind of person I want to be?"

The second important thing about sin is that it is a social act, that is, an act that affects those around us. Today it is fashionable to speak of a "right to privacy," which implies that certain actions have no real moral impact on family, society or nation. But if we believe, as the Catholic moral tradition does, that people are inherently connected with one another, then few of my acts are absolutely private and without social implications. And at some level, there is a further reality we call "social sin," which is the cumulative effect of individual sins.

We might say that as individuals we can't do anything about social structures that deprive people of rights or housing or employment. Cultural attitudes and social structures become complex and sometimes get out of our control. But they are still human creations and they can be changed. The institution of slavery, once deeply embedded in our culture, has disappeared. Attitudes toward the death penalty are changing. India, shaken by a violent gang rape that resulted in the death of a young woman in 2013, is beginning to examine the cultural attitudes about women that contributed to this violence. So our responsibility extends not just to "doing good acts," ourselves, nor even to "becoming certain kinds of persons." It also involves standing back and assessing our world as objectively as we can.

What about Confession?

Confession raises a lot of questions. Does the decline in the frequency of confession mean that sin has disappeared and that no one takes sin seriously anymore? Is confession a humiliating experience? Are some sins so bad they can't be forgiven? If I haven't been to confession in a long time, where do I start?

If we see sin as a choice of a lesser good and as a diminishment of who we are as persons, then confession becomes a kind of spiritual therapy. Far from being an encounter with an authority who judges us and "absolves" us of our sins, reconciliation becomes a healing moment when we face our own limitations, and try to broaden our vision and choice so that we always choose the greatest good possible. The grace of the sacrament allows us to see our own sinfulness and to know that we can do better.

The decline in frequent confession may not be an entirely bad thing. Seeing confession as a time to recite a "laundry list" of sins week after week may trivialize sin, and make it appear that we are just confessing little mistakes. If we go to confession somewhat less frequently, but with a deeper awareness of sin as a tendency, an inclination, and a state which needs to be healed, we might benefit more from it. Such an approach might help us remember that sin is not just "what we do," but "who we choose to become."

This healing does not happen all at once, and most of us will be plagued by the same sins – tendencies to choose the same short-term goods – over and over again. But confession provides us with the opportunity to face those limitations and to keep trying to "choose better," even if our choices only improve in fits and starts.

If you haven't been to confession in a long time, don't worry. Make an appointment with a priest or simply step into the confessional and tell him that it has been a long time. Then start with why you are there. He will help you through the rest.

A wise therapist once told me that we should not expect therapy to turn us into different persons. If, for example, I look at myself as a strong solid oak tree, it would be unrealistic to expect myself to be transformed into a beautiful but fragile flowering crab. Similarly, reconciliation must aim at helping us be "better as who we are" – not changing radically overnight, but discovering our strengths, our best sides and our gifts and allowing grace to enhance them. More like pruning and trimming than uprooting, confession should perfect what God has given us rather than destroy it.

Chapter 7 – Let the Virtues Be Your Guide

"Virtue," said Mark Twain, "has never been as respectable as money." What Twain was no doubt referring to is the fact that most of us find it easier to judge people on the basis of what they *have or do* than on the basis of *who they are*. People who have amassed huge fortunes or build large businesses or own impressive homes or cars earn a certain immediate respect from those they meet. Those whose material possessions or accomplishments are more modest but who are people of deep integrity, honest or compassion earn our respect much more slowly. Yet morality has far more to do with these latter qualities than with merely having or doing. How would I want others to describe me? As a person of great wealth, or as a person who is impeccably honest? As someone who has several thousand employees, or as someone known for justice and compassion?

We have already shown how through much of Christian history morality was described primarily in terms of the virtues: flexible qualities of character which shape inclinations and dispositions to act in certain ways. At one point of history, the study of virtue was neglected in favor of a more legalistic approach to morality which was concerned not so much with the cultivation of these qualities of character, but with adherence to the law. Not that law is a bad thing. We need laws to guide us and show us the way. But morality and law are not the same thing. Law compels and directs from the outside, whereas morality (and virtue) grow from within, shaping the very core of who we are. This is evident from the fact that it is possible to keep the letter of the law while flagrantly and willfully violating its spirit. Take the example of a businessman who scrupulously adheres to the state employment regulations, but uses loopholes in the law the dismiss employees before they are eligible for pensions. As long as he stays within the requirements of the law he could not be accused of a crime, but we would certainly not consider him a man of sound moral character.

What is Virtue?

Many years ago an article was written entitled "Virtue is Not a Habit."[6] The title was ironic, because properly understood, a *habit* is exactly what a virtue is. What the author of the article meant was that virtue is not a habit in the sense we usually understand the term, i.e., something we do unconsciously or involuntarily, like biting our fingernails or tapping our fingers on the desk. We remain blissfully unaware of it until someone calls our attention to it. A *moral habit* (the word comes from the Latin word *habitus*) is any kind of activity that is very consciously cultivated and nurtured, until it becomes almost second nature. Quite unlike nervous, unconscious habits, *moral habits* are those skills which are developed over time, training our human capacities to respond readily and happily in a certain way. These moral habits are like the ability acquired by athletes or musicians who practice for years at a time to be able to quickly and easily run a one-hundred yard dash in record time or play a difficult piece of music flawlessly and gracefully.

Like musical or athletic skills, virtues can be strengthened by frequent use; they can also weaken or disintegrate through neglect. They enable our human capacities of desiring, willing, thinking, feeling and judging to work together smoothly and to help us arrive at good moral decisions with ease. Let us take a look at four of the most important, or cardinal virtues: temperance, fortitude, justice and prudence.

Temperance: The Virtue of Consumers

Perhaps no virtue is more important in our society than temperance. Although often associated only with abstinence from alcohol, temperance is the virtue that moderates all of our desires, especially those of touch. Because we live in a market-driven, consumer society, we are almost never free from invitations to indulge our desires. These desires, even those of the flesh, are not necessarily wrong; temperance recognizes that these desires for physical pleasure and comfort are good. Our desire for good and beautiful things is at the very root of what morality means. But because of our human weakness, these desires must be properly trained.

Temperance seeks the middle road: neither too much sensual gratification (which results in the vices of gluttony and lust), nor too little (which results in a vice St. Thomas calls insensibility – the inability to desire anything – a kind of moral anesthesia whereby we have blunted or destroyed all our desires entirely.) This leaves only the shell of a human person, someone unable to enjoy anything, even God. Temperance teaches us to enjoy beauty and comfort and physical pleasure, but in a measured way appropriate to how we live our lives. Like the other virtues, it is flexible. What is "just enough" for me may be too much or too little for another person. The core of temperance is learning our limits and coming to recognize when our need for gratification begins to obscure other important values in our lives.

An important aspect of temperance is that it also regulates desire for the satisfaction of knowing things we don't need to know or for vengeance or anger. We consider gossip as a vice because it is rooted in an intemperate desire to know things about other people. Intemperate anger, especially if it leads to vengeance, is also a vice. While it might feel good to really "let someone have it," especially if they deserve it, it is often intemperate to indulge that desire.

Fortitude: Remedy for Fear

Unlike temperance, which helps us moderate desires for pleasure and comfort, fortitude helps us moderate our *fear* and enables us to overcome our weakness and anxiety in the pursuit of good things. Often referred to as the virtue of martyrs and soldiers, who are called upon to be courageous in the face of danger, fortitude also comes in a more everyday variety which teaches us to overcome the routine fears that plague all of us as we try to live good lives. Courage is important, especially at a time when the media makes us aware of every threat, local and global. As New York Times columnist Scott Shane says,

> "As terrorist plots against the US have piled up, politicians and the news media have sounded the alarm with a riveting message: Be afraid. Al Qaeda is on the march again, targeting the country from within and without, and your hapless government cannot protect you...." [7]

Without courage, we are simply overwhelmed, personally and politically. As Scott Bader-Saye notes in his book, *Following Jesus in a Culture of Fear*,

> The disposition to view one's existence as being at risk has a discernible effect on the conduct of life. It causes us to shrink from greatness, it disposes us to panic, leads to a dread of strangers and diminishment of trust. It leads to a world view that equates the good life with self-limitation and risk aversion.

One area in which many of us lack fortitude is in the area of commitments. While few of us deny that commitments are good things, we often fail to make them because we are afraid: Fear of criticism, fear of failure, fear of physical harm, fear of intimacy, fear of disappointment, fear of humiliation all stand in the way of our commitments we make to good things. Fear is natural. But when we allow fear to limit our pursuit of the good excessively, we back ourselves into a smaller and smaller corner until at last we are afraid to go after anything we value.

While it is often easier to simply give in rather than wage the fight for something we believe in, fortitude strengthens us and helps us overcome obstacles that stand in our way. Fortitude helps us see beyond our fears and take reasonable risks to secure what we know is good. Like temperance, fortitude seeks the mean: those who take foolish risks are called foolhardy; those who take no risks, even for very great goods, are called cowards.

Justice: Our Life in Community

Justice is unique. Unlike the other moral virtues, it is specifically concerned with our relationships with others. This is why the term "social justice" is redundant. Virtues that moderate personal qualities like anger or desire are more individual. Justice is inherently social and moderates our life together. While temperance controls my desire, and fortitude controls my anger, justice controls my life in community.

We probably hear more explicit references to justice than to any of the other virtues. Congressional scandals, savings and loan frauds, welfare, divorce, economics, and allocation of medical care are all involve questions of justice. Justice is a public virtue which orders our relationships to those around us. It tries to assure that "each one receives according to his or her due." When we say that something is unjust, we mean that someone was deprived of something due them: often money or goods, but also truth, fidelity, or respect.

There are three kinds of justice, each dealing with certain kinds of relationships among people. *Distributive* justice deals with what the *whole* (often society) owes to the *parts* (individual citizens.) The most obvious example of distributive justice is in the allocation of social goods like education, police protection, fire, water and sewer, and medical care. In each of these instances, justice determines how common goods should be distributed among many people with claims upon them. In disputed cases, judges and courts sometimes have to intervene.

Another kind of justice deals with the obligation of the *parts to the whole*. Taxes, by which individual citizens contribute to the common good, are the most obvious example of this kind of justice. As soon as we become part of a group, we owe something to that group. Membership, as one credit card company reminds us, may have privileges, but it also has responsibilities. *Legal justice* dictates how much each individual part owes to the whole.

Finally, *commutative justice* deals with the relationship of the *parts to one another*. When a young couple buys a new house, for example, they may execute a contract on that house, agreeing to pay a certain amount of money in exchange for possession of the house. Any kind of agreement like this constitutes an example of commutative justice, which regulates relationships among individuals. Taking someone to court for breach of contract or for failure to repay a loan both involve appeals to commutative justice.

Becoming just involves deepening our awareness that we are not merely individuals but parts of larger groups: families, villages, cities, states, nations and now, a global community. As soon as we become part of these groups, justice comes into play. Our membership in these groups places certain responsibilities upon us, and it guarantees us certain privileges, or rights. Justice advocates often speak about rights, but it is very important to remember that for every right there is a corresponding responsibility upon someone else. So when we speak of a "right to housing" or a "right to education" or even a "right to life" we must ask, "Upon whom does this right place a claim?"

Purely abstract rights which place no specific responsibility upon anyone are empty. The "right to life" and the "right to privacy," about which we hear so much today are what we call negative rights: Unlike the right to education, which asks *for* something, rights to privacy and life ask to *be free* from something, namely, interference. But in all three cases, we must ask, "Upon whom does this right place a claim?" Who has the responsibility to provide education? Society? The Church? The federal government? Or, who has the responsibility leave me, or this child, free from interference? Remembering that justice always requires at least two parties – the one making the claim and the one filling it - makes seemingly intractable debates about justice issues easier to solve.

Prudence: The Heart of the Virtuous Life

We think of a "prude" as someone who is timid and afraid. Yet prudence is a strong virtue which permeates all the rest of the virtues and which helps us make specific choices in concrete circumstances. It involves practical knowing, that is, it is not merely speculation, but *what-is-to-be-done-in-this-case*. Professionals like doctors and lawyers have to be prudent because they apply general rules or principles to specific cases of medicine or law. Far from being just restraint, prudence also involves daring, imagination and creativity. From the many artistic representations of prudence, one of the most interesting is a 16th century sculpture which portrays virtue as a person with two faces. One face is that of an old man with a flowing beard, representing the wisdom, experience and judiciousness of prudence; the other face is that of a young a lovely woman, representing prudence's flexibility, innovation and freshness.

Prudence has several steps:

Memory. First of all, the prudent person must learn to remember past experience, especially experiences similar to the one he or she is facing at the moment. The old adage "Experience is the best teacher" is appropriate here. Remembering similar situations from the past can help us do better in the present.

Foresight. Prudence also requires that we be able to see what's ahead, especially possible obstacles or consequences to proposed courses of action. Something might look like a good choice until we examine all of its possible ramifications; its weaknesses then become apparent.

Imagination. Cartoons sometimes illustrate characters who have a good idea by a light bulb above their heads. The "illumination" which this image suggests is crucial to good decision making. While memory and foresight are helpful in gathering knowledge, we also need to be able to put it together and discover creative solutions to difficult problems. Imagination in the moral life helps us to see possibilities that might not have occurred to us at first. It helps us make connections between the good we seek and the situation with we are faced right now. Truly prudent persons are those to whom we would turn to get insightful, imaginative solutions to difficult problems.

Docility is the last important quality of prudence. Docility does not mean submission, but openness or willingness to learn. All the memory, foresight and imagination in the world will do us no good at all unless we are willing to be instructed or taught by it. Particularly important here is openness to the experience of others. Those who are older than us can frequently bring experience that is far beyond our own. Seeking counsel from others and allowing that counsel to shape our course of action is a key quality of prudence.

The moral virtues concern not the end of our lives, which is friendship and union with God, but the means to achieve that union. This friendship, which we call charity, is the form of the virtues; that is, it is the reason the virtues exist: to help us become closer to God through love of him. By temperance, fortitude, justice and temperance, we are made fully human, and that makes us fully open to God's grace, uniting us with him in friendship.

Friendship is an important moral quality in itself. In many ways, the virtuous life could be said to be a life of friendship: when we achieve virtue, the various parts of our personalities (our desires, fears, needs, judgment, emotions, etc.) befriend one another and create a deep tranquility and quality of life. That tranquility in turn enables us to befriend others – to form friendships with others and to give birth to a just society.

Chapter 8 – Liturgy and the Moral Life

We have described virtues as moral qualities or skills which are developed over the course of a lifetime. As such, they are nourished and fostered by our life of prayer and worship. The great cathedrals of Europe, for instance, frequently had stained glass windows or sculptures portraying the virtues (one of these, a sculpture of the virtue of prudence from the Cathedral of Amiens, appears on the cover of this book). They were meant to remind the faithful that liturgy was a "school for virtue" which taught us who we should be through music, art and preaching.

I once heard the confession of a woman who had been away from the Church for many years. After our discussion, I suggested that she attend a special mass the parish was celebrating that night. She asked me, "Is that my penance?" She had seen some connection between morality and liturgy, but it was the wrong one. She saw mass as a punishment or reparation for all the years she had been away from the church. I intended it as a healing, reconciling event, a kind of "moral lift" which would be the first step in helping her begin her life anew.

The Connection between Morality and Liturgy

We don't often associate morality with liturgy, except inasmuch as we are required by church law to attend mass on Sundays and certain other days. But in fact, the church's liturgy, and especially the Eucharist, are at the root of a solid moral life. That is so because both morality and liturgy involve dialogue, remembrance, inspiration, transformation and friendship. Let us explore each of these in turn.

Dialogue. One of my earliest memories as a Catholic was learning the Latin responses to the mass when I became an altar boy. When the priest said, "*Introibo ad altare Dei,*" I learned to respond, "*Ad Deum qui laetificat juventutem meum.*" At the time I didn't know what those words meant, nor did I know that I was substituting for the entire congregation. The Eucharist was a dialogue between the priest and the people, and that dialogue was meant to symbolize that the Eucharist was a participatory event. It is not a spectator sport, something done to us or for us, but something in which we are all intimate participants.

The same is true of morality. Sometimes morality seems to be a matter of someone else imposing behavior upon us. But the moral life is a dialogue between me and God, between me and community as I shape my life. Much as the liturgical assembly sings, responds, stands, sits, and processes in unity, so we shape our moral lives with other people and in dialogue with them. In one sense it is true to say that morality is a private matter, because I alone bear the responsibility for my free decisions. But in another way, morality is very much a communal event which requires the help and insight of many other people. The goal of the moral life should be to achieve some kind of harmony with those around us.

Remembering. All of our liturgical actions involve remembering. When we go to Mass, for example, we listen to the Word of the Lord, which often recalls what God has done for us. When we pray the Eucharistic prayer, we remember the living and the dead in prayer and we recall the example of Mary and the saints. Most importantly, we remember Jesus' death and resurrection, ("Christ has died...Christ has risen...Christ will come again"). This remembering is of a special kind, so powerful that it actually makes these events present here and now.

The moral life involves remembering, too. As we approach moral decisions we must remember the moral teaching of the scriptural word, our own past experience and the experience of the saints and others around us. In remembering we strengthen our faith and our resolve to "do better next time."

Inspiration. Just at the middle of the Eucharistic prayer, the priest says, "Lord, let your spirit come upon these gifts and make them holy..." Those words call God's life-giving spirit not only upon the bread and wine, but upon the congregation as well. It is the Spirit whose presence makes Christ alive among us, which draws us together and binds us into one spiritual family.

The Holy Spirit is of vital importance to the moral life, too. Often when we think of the gifts of the Holy Spirit, we think of what Christopher Kiesling referred to as the "noisy" gifts – prophecy, healing, baptism in the Spirit, slaying in the Spirit. But the moral life is animated by other gifts – the "quiet" ones such as wisdom and understanding, right judgment, courage, knowledge and reverence. Even when we have carefully trained our abilities to help us live justly, temperately, and so forth, we have never done quite enough. These gifts of the Holy Spirit are the finishing touches on our moral lives, filling them out and perfecting them. In some ways, our own efforts at morality can be compared to the work of a carpenter who "frames out" a new house. All the beams, joists and angles are there and make a sturdy and durable base. But the Gifts of the Spirit are like the work the cabinet maker, painter and decorator does. They finish the house off and make it livable and beautiful. Like subtle finishes on fine furniture, these gifts are not obtrusive and we must learn to recognize them and appreciate them. Learning to recognize these gifts involves a special openness each time the priest invokes the Spirit upon the Eucharistic gifts, for that Spirit touches us as well.

Transformation. Perhaps the most dramatic similarity between liturgy and morality is *transformation.* No one who has ever witnessed a baptism at the Easter vigil can fail to be touched by the movement from darkness to light, or by the passing of the newly baptized through the water of salvation and into a clean white robe. These things are both signs of the transformation from death to life which takes place at baptism. Similarly, when we pray the Eucharistic prayer at mass, we hear the priest say, "This is my body...This is my blood." In so doing, he announces the transformation not only of the bread and wine, but of the whole assembly. All of us who have been baptized have been brought into the body of Christ, and each time these words are spoken, the spirit hovers over us and over the gifts of bread and wine, transforming them all into Christ's own body.

If we focus on the Eucharistic elements only, we can lose sight of this dramatic mystery. It is important for us to recall that the essence of the moral life is transformation. Just as in the Eucharist we take ordinary elements of bread and wine, in morality we take the ordinary, unformed and incomplete elements of our lives. And just as the Eucharistic action transforms that ordinary bread and wine into the Body and Blood of Christ, so it transforms our ordinary lives into increasingly perfect lives of virtue and grace. The wonder of the Eucharist and of the moral life is not just that it *is*, but that it *becomes.* What was once purely human and imperfect becomes, though the action of the assembly and the movement of the spirit, a reflection of God's own self. So the Eucharistic prayer should focus us not only on the altar, but should lead us to feel God's transforming power *within ourselves.*

Friendship. As Jesus hints when he says, "I no longer call you servants, but friends," our relationship with God is a kind of friendship. At times this seems impossible to us, because of the great distance that exists between us as humans and God who made us. Yet even after the act of creation, God remains so close to us and so intimately involved in our lives that it is not an exaggeration for us to say that the spirituality and morality are a matter of building a friendship with God.

The philosopher Aristotle says that there are three kinds of friendship. The first is *useful* friendship, which we cultivate because it can bring us some good. Friendships in business are sometimes of this sort. Business people become friends because their relationship can be of mutual benefit. They might not spend social time together, but they are friends because they have a mutual interest in their work. A second kind of friendship is one that is *pleasurable*; there are some people to whom we are drawn because of some quality within them which pleases us, such as wittiness or a sense of humor. We enjoy being around these people because they make us feel good, and we would consider them to be "friends" in a certain way. These kinds of friendship can be unstable, however, because they are based either upon some benefit to be gotten or some enjoyable quality. If the benefit or the quality disappears, the friendship may, as well.

There is a third kind of friendship which is based neither on usefulness nor pleasure. It derives instead from the goodness that two people see in each other. This is the deepest kind of friendship, but also the most difficult to attain. Often we are attracted to people on the basis of what they can give us, or because of the pleasure we get from associating with them; but in time, we may begin to see the deeper inner goodness and a true, lasting friendship begins to form. This is the kind of friendship we have with God. God befriends us not because we can give him anything or because we amuse him, but because he sees our deepest intrinsic goodness. We may be initially attracted to God because of what we think we can get (e.g., salvation or holiness). As we grow in faith we begin to realize that we love God because of his goodness, and true mutual friendship begins to develop.

Just like our friendships with other people, our friendship with God develops slowly and sometimes in fits and starts. But because they are rooted in seeking the truly good in others and sharing our goodness with them, these friendships are the basis of the moral life: being moral, or truly happy, means discovering true values of honesty, intelligence, charity, truthfulness, compassion and strength in our friends; in return, we cultivate our own virtues so that we become more attractive to those we wish to befriend. True friends engage in a kind of covenant by which they agree to draw the very best out of each other. It is almost like two athletes who train together: they are able to see and correct one another's weaknesses, exhort one another to better performance, and share one another's victories, all the while improving themselves, too. Far from being one-sided, our relationship with God is like this, too. Though it is difficult to say that we help God "improve," God wants our love and gratitude. For example, God needs us to help realize his plan for the world. In return, God gives us his Spirit which strengthens us and makes us holy.

Aristotle notes that friendship is at once "a state, an activity and a feeling." This reminds us that while we can be friends, and feel friendship, we must also cultivate friendship by certain kinds of activities. Friends mark their friendship by sharing meals, celebrating special events and just spending quiet time together. Similarly, as we befriend God, we share the Eucharistic meal, celebrate special moments like marriage, birth and death, and sometimes just spend quiet time together, in prayer. St. Thomas Aquinas notes that "for friends to converse together is the proper condition of friendship. Our conversation with God is through contemplation." So when we pray quietly, we are really conversing with God, coming to know him better, appreciating his goodness and allowing him to appreciate ours. As we do this, we begin to see reflections of God's own goodness in those around us. We are drawn to that goodness in others not merely because it is useful or pleasurable, but because it is holy – and this becomes the basis for our friendships with others.

It would be difficult to underestimate the importance of friendship to the moral life. As Paul Waddell says in his marvelous book *The Primacy of Love*, "Friendships constitute our lives. Friends are those who, through their loving attention to us, sculpt us to wholeness… A good friend is someone who draws the best out of us, someone who creates us in the most promising way." The importance of friends to our moral lives is obvious if we see the moral life as becoming the best possible persons we can be. Since we are often blind to much of our own goodness, friends help one another to see that goodness and make it real.

The Trinity as a Model of Friendship

In the 15th century, a famous artist named Rublev painted one of the world's best known icons. It shows three identical figures seated around a table. These three persons symbolize the Trinity, and their meal symbolizes the friendship among them. But the table has an empty space, directly in front of the viewer. That empty space suggests that the Trinity invites us into their friendship to share their own life and joy. The essence of our moral and liturgical lives is accepting this invitation and learning to imitate the friendship of the Trinity in our relationships with others.

PART III – FACING TODAY'S MORAL DILEMMAS

Chapter 9 – Health Care Reform: Our Social Responsibility

With this chapter, we move from a relatively abstract discussion of the "foundations" of Christian morality to a more detailed discussion of some specific moral problems which face our society today. Each of the following discussions will try to provide conscience formation on a particular issue. These chapters will not necessarily reach conclusions (that is the role of conscience), but they will provide some of the tools necessary to reach decisions.

There are two major aspects of health care ethics. The first is concerned with *social ethics,* which helps us as a society deal with the big questions about health care.

The second area concerns moral choices about my own care or the care of someone else for whom I have legal or familial responsibility. We will start with the social issues because the way we answer the big questions will determine the choices we have for our own personal care.

The Current State of Health Care in the United States

The U.S. has the most sophisticated and technically advanced health care in the world. It does not come cheap. We currently spend $2.6 trillion per year on health care or $8,402 for every man, woman and child in the country. This amount has been steadily rising in total dollars and in per capita expenditures for many years. In 1970, we spent $356 per person on health care annually. Our total expenditures were 7.2% of our gross domestic product. In 2010, they had risen to

17.9% of the GDP. We spend at least twice as much as any other country, yet outcomes in critical areas like longevity and infant mortality are no better than in countries that spend far less. In fact, in some areas our outcomes are significantly worse than countries that spend less.[8]

How Do We Pay for Health Care?

The debate about health care reform is primarily about quality and access, but there are also serious problems with the way we finance health care. For many years, we have relied on three main sources of funding: Medicare, Medicaid and private insurance.

Medicare was inaugurated in the 1960s as a way of providing basic health care to those over 65. It has functioned reasonably well, but it has grown with the cost and complexity of health care itself. Today it threatens to overwhelm the premiums paid by working and retired persons. There are gaps in its coverage which must be filled by private supplemental insurance or by other government entitlement programs. In 2010 it provided coverage for about 20% of the population.

Medicaid was mandated by the government as a means of providing health care to the poor and disabled, and it is run by the various states. This causes difficulties when particular states experience financial problems which prevent them from meeting all the coverage requirements established by the government. In addition, Medicare patients who do not have supplemental insurance must often fall back on Medicaid to cover things such as nursing home care when they are not reimbursed by Medicare. In 2010 about 15% of the population was covered by Medicaid.

Private insurance is the largest category of health care coverage, and is held by about 32% of the population. Of this group, many are covered by employer-provided health plans, and about 13% are covered by privately purchased, non-group insurance. These plans include *traditional insurance plans*, which grant patients complete freedom to choose physicians and health care facilities as well as *health maintenance organizations* (HMOs) and *preferred provider organizations* (PPOs) which place some restrictions on which doctors you may see or what hospitals or clinics you may use. Insurance tends to provide reimbursement on a "fee for services" basis and usually requires that the patient pay some expenses out of pocket in the form of a deductible. HMOs and PPOs usually provide coverage on a "capitation" basis, meaning that the patient or employer pays a single, "per capita" charge for coverage and receives no itemized bills.

Government-sponsored health care. Many Americans are unaware that the United States does have some forms of socialized health care. Both the Veterans' Health Administration and the Indian Health Service are closed systems that run parallel to our patchwork of private and public health. These two systems most closely resemble European-type systems because they are owned and funded entirely by the government. Physicians are actually government employees. Although they serve limited populations they have some very innovative programs and provide comprehensive and integrated health care. The Indian Health Service serves about 2.5 million patients a year and has a budget of $4 billion. The Veterans' Health Administration serves 8.3 million patients and has a budget of $47 billion. Together, they account for less than 1% of total spending.

It is also important to know that for decades the federal government has funded about 50% of all health care costs through a number of the programs mentioned above. There has been no dramatic increase in the government's share of overall expenditures.

Does Health Care Need Reform?

There are three reasons why health care needs reform in the United States. The first is economic sustainability. We have already shown the dramatic rise in health care spending both in real dollars and as a percentage of the gross domestic product. Research continues to identify new diseases and new therapies push up the cost of health care. If health care costs continue to rise at a rate faster than inflation, they will eventually overwhelm our economy and squeeze out funding for other basic goods like education and housing.

The second issue is coverage and access. If health care were just a commodity like real estate, automobiles or flat screen televisions, we could leave supply and demand to the market. Those who could afford a new car or an entertainment center would simply save up and buy one. Health care is different because health is an intrinsic value in the way no other product is. In addition, medical knowledge is not proprietary like the patents and inventions that make entertainment technology possible. Medical knowledge is the result of public and private financing, patient suffering and the altruism of volunteers who make medical experimentation possible. Medical knowledge is a social good that belongs to all of us. It is like the village commons of old: a field to which everyone contributed and from which everyone benefited.

Because healthcare is a basic human good and because it is the property of society, it must be distributed with relative equity. We will never get to the point where health care services are allocated with mathematical precision. There will always be some who can afford more or faster service, but we must work to assure that each citizen has access to a certain basic level of health care and protection from financial ruin if serious illness results.

Finally, our current system is inefficient. Good stewardship of our resources demands that we use these resources as efficiently as possible. Because of the complex payment system, we spend as much as 20% of our health care dollars on administrative costs. In 1999, for example, the US spent $1,059 per person on administrative costs compared to $307 in Canada.

How Should Catholics Think About Health Care Reform?

Catholic social teaching does not provide a detailed plan for health care reform, but it does offer several basic principles that can guide us. These principles have been clearly articulated by the US Bishops. In February 2013, the Bishops' website (www.usccb.org) provided a summary of their goals:

- a truly universal health policy with respect for human life and dignity;
- access for all with a special concern for the poor and inclusion of immigrants;
- pursuing the common good and preserving pluralism including freedom of conscience and variety of options;
- restraining costs and applying them equitably across the spectrum of payers.

The Catholic Health Association proposed a similar list it its advocacy agenda prior to the 2012 presidential election. (www.chausa.org).

Justice and the Right to Health Care

Citizens on both sides of the debate about health care reform argue for justice. Some see it as a matter of personal responsibility – each person should pay for his own care; others see it as a matter of corporate responsibility, especially for the poor, the young and the elderly.

Although the simplest definition of justice is "the will that each receive his or her due," the reality is far more complicated. Justice is a complex web of interdependent relationships. It involves individual rights, both the right to certain things (e.g., public safety and respect) and the right to be free of certain things (e.g., undue interference, assault, restrictions on faith or worship). Wherever there is a right, there must be a corresponding obligation on someone's part. For instance, I might insist that I have a right to a new car every year, but if there is no one who recognizes that right, it is meaningless. Opponents of increased access to health care sometimes argue that "the government can't pay for everything." But the right to health care falls not on government but on society as a whole.

Because health care is such a fundamental human good, health care is the responsibility of *society* – doctors, patients, tax payers, politicians, religious leaders – cooperating together in the achievement of the common good. Government may be *used by society* as a means to providing health care, but the responsibility for providing these basic goods falls squarely on us. We cannot abdicate that responsibility to government, but neither can we ignore the role of government in helping to bring this reality about.

One of the major questions in health care reform is whether there is a right to health care. If it is merely a product, then we would have to say no. But if it is a basic requirement of human flourishing, then for reasons we have outlined above, we would have to say yes. This does not mean that everyone has a right to unlimited care, but that everyone in a society has a right to as much care as is compatible with the same level of care for everyone else.

Is There a Right to Low Taxes?

Another rights issue is the right to be free of burdensome taxes. Because politics today is so complicated, many voters have fixated on the slogan "no new taxes" as though that would solve all our problems. Pledges not to raise taxes have resulted in reduced public funding for education, health care and public safety. In some cases, critical public services like police or fire protection have been cut or replaced by private services which only those of means can afford.

Everyone wants low taxes. Our tradition teaches that we should always allow for the greatest freedom possible, and that extends even to the freedom to earn and spend as we like. But our tradition also tells us that as members of a society we are part of a living social organism. We are "in solidarity" with one another; that is, we have more in common with one another than the economic and social differences that divide us. We have a responsibility to those around us, without whose cooperation we cannot eat, be educated or secure health care. Even as we keep taxes low, we must be realistic about the costs of keeping this social organism healthy. We must remember that we cannot simply opt for the benefits of society without incurring an obligation. I might speak of *my* right to health care, but in the end, it has to be *our* right to health care, for if even one of us is sick, all of us are diminished. When we enter into the health care reform debate, we need to set aside our own private interests and ask "What kind of health care do *we* need?" rather than "What kind of health care do *I* need?"

The Common Good

Taken together, these intersecting rights are the threads in a social fabric we call the common good. The Catechism describes the common good as "the sum total of social conditions which allow people, either as groups or as individuals, to reach their fulfillment more fully and more easily. The common good concerns the life of all. It calls for prudence from each, and even more from those who exercise the office of authority" (#1906). The common good is the set of political and economic circumstances that enable the development of individuals and the group; it is also a foreshadowing of the Reign of God and of God's own self, which is our ultimate common good. This is why the common good is not just a political reality. It is the goal of our whole lives, the ultimate good to which God calls us. Yet many Americans are suspicious of it. Some even label it as socialist. For Americans it is almost a foreign language that we struggle to adopt against a lifetime of the language of individualism and individual rights. Dan Callahan notes this problem when he says:

> There is an absence in this country of a solid common good tradition...the thought that we might have to ration health care in the name of the common good – even to ensure that others get a fair share – is objectionable to most Americans, and our politicians have not dared to talk about it. It is the medical equivalent of not-in-my-backyard...[9]

We will never get justice quite right nor will we experience the fullness of the common good on this earth, but we continue to struggle for it. Persons of good will may differ on the best way to achieve the common good – whether through government, private enterprise or a mixture of the two. But the centrality of the common good is not optional. It is an important obligation for all Catholics.

What about Rationing?

The "r-word" strikes terror into the hearts of our citizens. Merely the mention of rationing can stop reform efforts dead. Yet, as one author points out, it is not at all clear what this word means. Does rationing mean

> "that the providers ... third-party payers (or both) are not making available the health care that Americans seek? ... [or] that a conscious decision has been made by providers not to give this care because it is too expensive?...[or] that providers are not giving Americans all the services they demand because it has been deemed that some services are not medically necessary? [or] that because third-party payers refuse to reimburse providers, providers refuse to supply them? [or] that the need for health care exceeds the capabilities of our health care system, forcing a triage situation?"[10]

Unless we believe that a) we will never die and b) society's resources are unlimited, then we have to embrace some kind of rationing, or at least rationalization, in the way we allocate health care. Unfortunately, many Americans are trying to entertain both of these fantasies. We refuse to accept the fact of human mortality and we also refuse to admit that we simply cannot afford every health care therapy for everyone.

Options for Reform

The current system is unethical because it distributes commonly held resources unjustly and according to ability to pay rather than according to need. It is also economically unsustainable because of its rapidly rising cost and because of our inability to accept limits. At this point, minor adjustments will not make any significant difference.

There are only a few ways to really change the way we fund health care. One would be to adopt socialized medicine, where the government owns and funds all health care services, like the British Health Service. Another would be to retain our hospitals and independent physicians but to have a single payer at a state or federal level. This is like Canada's system. Another approach would be a public-private mix with private hospitals and subsidies to help the poor buy private insurance. Some European countries have systems like this. A public-private mix seems to be the only approach Americans would find palatable.

The Affordable Care Act of 2010

There have been many health care reform proposals. The earliest one was set forth by Franklin Roosevelt in 1942. Harry Truman proposed a single-payer system in 1945. Bill Clinton unsuccessfully proposed the Health Security Act in 1993. None have gotten much traction, mostly because of fear of cost, fear of rationing, or fear of government involvement.

The proposals which appear to have the most support in are those which retain elements of competition, which Americans believe makes everything better, while trying to "manage" it in a constructive way. This would be accomplished by the establishment of a minimum standard health care package which would then be offered by a variety of competing companies and purchased by employers. Competition would be "managed" by standardizing policy benefits and assuring "guaranteed issue" of insurance to all who seek it, regardless of age or pre-existing conditions. The weakness of these proposals is that they place a heavy burden on employers, who would either have to "play" by purchasing health insurance or health coverage through HMOs or PPOs or their own programs, or pay a special tax which would provide coverage for their employees.

In 2010, Congress narrowly passed a bill proposed by the Obama Administration which would combine some elements of all the above approaches. The ACA is a wide-ranging and complicated initiative that would result in enormous changes in the way we finance health care. It aims to increase access, lower out-of-pocket costs, improve value, and change current provider payment incentives so that they encourage *higher quality* care rather than *more* care. Key provisions of the Act include:

Expanding Medicaid. This would extend coverage to individuals who make up to 138% of the Federal Poverty Level ($15,415 for individuals and $38,809 for a family of four). This would provide coverage, although at low reimbursement rates for providers, for the poorest citizens.

The Mandate: This is the most controversial part of the bill. It would require everyone to purchase medical insurance so that risk could be spread around more and theoretically the cost of insurance would be lower all around. It would also eliminate "cherry picking" in which insurance companies offer coverage only to the healthiest patients while leaving the poor, elderly and sick to public or charity care.

Health Insurance Exchanges: These insurance marketplaces would offer standard, comparable plans enabling patients to shop for the coverage that best suits them. Subsidies in the form of tax credits would provide assistance to those who could not afford the full cost of premiums.

Accountable Care Organizations (ACOs). These organizations might be run by insurance companies, clinics or groups of hospitals. They would not just provide care on demand as they do now. Rather they would assume responsibility for the health of a given population. This means that they would be accountable for preventing illness as well as treating it. ACOs would be penalized if they did not achieve good outcomes. For example, if a patient were readmitted to the hospital after treatment for a preventable problem, the hospital would not be reimbursed for the second admission. While brilliant in theory, ACOs will require a major shift in the way we think about health care. Providers will not have to take account of factors that were formerly seen as beyond their control such as health habits and voluntary health risks like smoking and obesity.

Electronic Medical Records. Another key feature of the Affordable Care Act is development of electronic medical records. Providers are being encouraged with financial incentives to digitize their records. While the adoption of EMRs has not yet resulted in reduced cost, the hope is that eventually increased portability of patient records will result in fewer redundant tests, better follow-up, and more effective risk assessment. The vast amount of data that cam be collected about outcomes will also help us identify the most effective treatments and to eliminate those that do not prove to be effective.

The final shape of this bill is by no means clear. The bill itself is over 2,000 pages long and there will tens of thousands of pages of additional regulations before all is said and done. The bill is not perfect, but it is an important step toward better stewardship of this vital resource

Will Health Care Reform Impact our Catholic Institutions?

Catholic institutions have had a major role in shaping today's health care and we have a strong interest in seeing that our values are respected. One of the most important of these values is the sanctity of life, which touches reproduction, abortion and care of the elderly and dying. The substance of Catholic teaching on these issues is well known.

Many Catholics are concerned that our long-held respect for life will be weakened if health care reform gives a greater role to government. While the US Bishops support many goals of health care reform, including greater access and affordability, they fear that provisions of the bill may violate conscience or force Catholic institutions will be compelled to cooperate in funding schemes that provide contraception or sterilization. As Cardinal George said in a 2010 statement:

> Two basic principles, therefore, continue to shape the concerns of the Catholic bishops: health care means taking care of the health needs of all, across the human life span; and the expansion of health care should not involve the expansion of abortion funding and of polices forcing everyone to pay for abortions.[11]

More recently the debate has expanded to include the possibility that Catholic institutions will be required to offer insurance coverage for contraception or that they will have to cooperate with others to facilitate provision of contraception. This too is viewed by the Church as an unacceptable compromise.

Two Moral Languages

The fact that Catholicism is a large "public" church creates a dilemma for us. On the one hand, our concern for the common good requires that we be actively involved in discussions about how society provides basic human goods like health care. On the other, we want to preserve the integrity of our convictions. As we do so, however, we must remember that our views on these matters do not stem primarily from our religious faith. That is, we do not believe abortion, sterilezation and euthanasia are wrong only because Revelation tells us so, but because we see these acts as inherently harmful to us as human persons. In a sense we can say that Catholics speak two moral languages: a religious or biblical language which says, "this act is wrong because it is an affront to the image of God within me." But we also have a language of reason or philosophy by which we can say, "this act is wrong because it is inhuman, it violates what it means to be a person."

Even those who do not share our religious faith can speak that language with us and dialogue about how the dignity of the human person might be realized. This dialogue is sometimes a messy, exasperating process. Few people deny the reality of human dignity, but there can be legitimate disagreements on the best way to protect it. Sometimes our involvement in this dialogue will require compromise as other persons of good will disagree with us about the best way in which to promote human dignity.

Since health care is a central part of the common good, we are bound to enter into the dialogue and to argue our view of human good as cogently and sincerely as we can. In the interest of securing the best overall health care for all of us, we may have to settle for less than 100% of our understanding of how best to protect that dignity. Practically, this may mean that we have to tolerate procedures we find objectionable in some public facilities in exchange for readily accessible care for children and the elderly while we also continue to persuade other citizens of the truth of our convictions.

Spirituality and Health Care Reform

Health care reform is a spiritual as well as an economic challenge. Because we are created "in the image of God," and because Christ became incarnate in a human body, our bodies are sacraments or "Temples of the Holy Spirit." This means that they actually reveal God to us and to others, and that we experience grace through our bodies rather than in spite of them. Our bodies are not just shells which hold our spirits, but are mysterious realizations of the power and love of God. Serious illness can provide us with an experience of the redemptive power of suffering. But it also impedes our work, our relationships, and our prayer. It can cause serious depression and make us lose interest in everything we hold dear. This makes health care, which preserves and heals the human body, unlike any other kind of human service.

Health Care as Sacramental

Because health care touches us at such a profound level of our existence, it has a deeply sacramental dimension to it. In Catholicism, the "sacramental principle" says that good and authentic things can be "occasions of grace." In addition to the seven sacraments with which we are all familiar, other deeply human things have the ability to mediate grace as well. The dedication and care of a skillful nurse, the procedures of a skilled surgeon, the patient efforts of a physical therapist, or the consoling words of friends all have the potential to bring grace into our lives. Indeed, physicians often have the experience of seeing effects of their treatments that they know they were not responsible for. God uses medical care in a way that makes his saving will tangible to us.

Chapter 10 – Personal Responsibility for Health Care

Medicine and medical care provide a special challenge for conscience. The requirements for a "good" conscience, are full knowledge, freedom and consent of the will. Medicine has probably advanced more in the last fifty years than in all of previous human history combined, and the range of medical knowledge and possible treatment options can seem overwhelming to even the most subtly formed conscience. Just a few of the questions which medicine poses to us today are the following:

How do I decide on treatment options for myself?

How do I decide *for others,* e.g., infants or the elderly, who are unable to choose and for whom I am responsible?

How do medical specialists decide how to allocate limited medical resources such as emergency rooms, hospital beds and specialized procedures?

How do *societies* decide what portion of social resources should be allocated to health care as opposed to other important social needs such as defense, education, city planning and police protection?

Whose responsibility is it to provide health care? Should it be equally available to all, or must it be rationed in some way? And if so, by whom?

This last question is perhaps the most difficult one which we face in the United States today. Until now, medical care has been rationed much like any other commodity: if you have the money to pay for it (or someone to pay for you), it is available; if not, you have to do without. As I have already noted, I believe there is a "right" to health care much as there is a right to education, human dignity, freedom from assault and freedom of speech. It should not be rationed by the market (that is, by economics alone) but should be distributed as equally as possible *by society*. In fact, medical knowledge and resources are a social possession for which all of us have a responsibility. It does not "belong" to the government to do with as it pleases, nor does it "belong" to individual hospitals, doctors or medical care personnel. They hold it in trust for the rest of us, and it is up to all of us – doctors, patients, legislators, ordinary citizens and the church – to help determine how to make it justly accessible to all.

Although the questions surrounding medical ethics are complex ones, there are several principles that provide a basis for many ethical questions.

Patient autonomy and informed consent. We have already noted that conscience is the ability to know moral truth and to apply it to particular situations. In medical situations, this translates into what we call "patient autonomy," that is, the patient's right and obligation to make his own choices about medical care. *Informed consent* means that the patient understands her condition and the available treatment options, and is able to make a reasonably intelligent choice about them. Informed consent involves three things: knowledge, competence (the ability to deliberate about choices) and freedom from coercion or manipulation. This last aspect is particularly important in the case of the elderly, who are sometimes placed under pressure by their families to choose one or another course of action. Their freedom to choose can be limited in obvious ways like overmedication and physical restraint, or in more subtle ways like wistful glances or sighs from family members, excessive encouragement or silence by physicians and other health care personnel.

Informed consent is not the same thing as a consent form. Informed consent is a moral choice which may be ratified by a signature on a consent form; but it is not once-and-for-all and must be considered flexible: that is, it must often be sought and given anew, especially in long-term care or therapy, as the patient's condition and prognosis change.

Finally, while the patient herself has primary responsibility for health care decisions, informed consent is not a solitary exercise. Because medical care decisions are so complex, and because they often have implications for family and friends, they should really be family decisions and should flow from the patient's partnership with the physician who often understands the patient's condition, prognosis and options better than the patient can. While the physician usually does not decide *for* the patient, neither should she be a passive bystander who only provides objective information. Informed consent should be the result of a *dialogue* among patient, physician and family, and should always be open to revision.

Specific Treatment Decisions

After it has been determined that necessary conditions for informed consent are present, specific treatment decisions must be made. Generally, the Catholic tradition has talked about these in terms of "ordinary and extraordinary means." *Ordinary* means are those which we are obliged to undergo, while *extraordinary* means are those which we may legitimately forego. There is no textbook or list which describes which procedures or treatments are "ordinary," nor are they classified merely according to their cost, complexity or availability.

Whether a treatment is ordinary or extraordinary is determined by a kind of balancing act between *benefits and burdens:* when faced with a decision to undergo chemotherapy for cancer, for example, we must weigh the expected benefits – whether the chances are good that it will result in an improvement of our condition – against the burdens – the pain, expense, anxiety and cost. And that calculation can change. For example, chemotherapy may be "ordinary" in the first occurrence of cancer, when cancer recurs or spreads to other parts of the body, a patient may decide that *at this point* the burdens of another course of chemotherapy have become too great to justify the benefits. This is where the flexibility of the notion of ordinary and extraordinary distinction comes in. The balance is not the same for every patient and change in the patient's condition or state of mind may change the balance between benefit and burden. What is "ordinary" for me, as a relatively healthy 60-year old man, for example, might be extraordinary – morally non-obligatory – for an 85-year old man suffering from congestive heart failure, cancer and diabetes.

One particularly challenging aspect of medical choice is that of *proxy judgment,* where the patient is not able to exercise informed consent for himself. This may be because of non-competence, as in the case of an infant who has never had the ability to choose, or incompetence, in the case of someone who at one time did have the ability to choose but lost it, either temporarily or permanently, because of illness. In these cases, someone else (usually the next-of-kin) exercises that power for the patient.

This may be done in one of two ways. If the patient's wishes are known, the proxy tries to *duplicate those wishes* as closely as possible. We might call this "substituted judgment." If the patient's wishes are not known, which is the case with infants or with young people who have never had occasion to discuss such things, the proxy makes a decision on the basis of the patient's best interests; in other words, the next-of-kin try to make the burdens/benefits judgment for the patient, because the patient's own wishes are not known.

In 1990, Congress addressed the growing complexity of medical decision-making when it enacted the Patient Self Determination Act. This legislation requires that all patients be notified of their right to make their own health care choices, to accept or refuse treatment, and to provide for advance health care directives in the event that they are not able to choose for themselves.

Advance directives are of two kinds. *Living wills*, which are implemented as soon as death threatens, specify in advance what choices the patient would want made. Living wills are limited, however, by language and terms which vary from state to state. A *durable power of attorney* becomes effective as soon as one is incapable of medical decision-making even if the patient is not in danger of death. It assigns primary responsibility for making medical decisions to someone you trust: spouse, child, parent or friend. Now recognized in many states, these durable powers of attorney give your delegate the power to decide for you if you are unable to do so yourself.

The advantage of a durable power of attorney over a living will is that it avoids having to specify in detail all the possible medical situations that might arise. Instead, it gives general decision making authority to one person, who can then exercise informed consent for you if you are incapacitated. But it also requires that the person delegated to make decisions for you knows and understands your wishes. Used correctly, durable powers of attorney can help keep medical decision making in the family and close to the patient, where it should be.

A *Physician Order for Life Sustaining Treatment* (POLST) is yet another option that has been adopted by many states. Usually printed on brightly colored paper, it gives the patient the opportunity to specify what kinds of treatments are desired. The POLST is designed to instruct emergency personnel on what kinds of treatments you want if you have a medical emergency while you while you're still at home or in the emergency room. Without it, emergency personnel are required to provide all possible treatments. The POLST complements the Advance Directive, which is necessary to appoint a legal representative and provide instructions hospital or nursing home personnel for future life-sustaining treatments, and is not intended to replace it.

No advance medical planning will work unless it is supported by candid discussion between the patient and the surrogate. These discussions should happen "early and often," especially for elderly patients whose condition may change frequently.

Foregoing and Withdrawing Life-Sustaining Treatment

The most difficult question we face in medical ethics today is whether it morally permissible to forego or withdraw life-sustaining treatments. From what we have said above, it is clear that the Catholic tradition holds that it is permissible to do so, provided the calculation of burdens and benefits has been made. There is no significant moral difference between stopping a treatment once it has been started and not starting it at all. Sometimes we feel that once a treatment has begun, it must be continued. But in fact, trial use of a treatment, in the hope that its benefits will be significant, may actually reveal it is ineffective and should be discontinued.

Special interest has been focused on cases in which the "treatment" is the artificial delivery of food and water to certain classes of permanently debilitated patients. While often loosely referred to as "comatose," these patients, like Nancy Cruzan in Missouri or Terry Schiavo in Florida, were actually in a different medical condition called PVS, or "persistent vegetative state." This means that because of physical trauma, lack of oxygen or drug use, most of the patient's brain has been so severely damaged that it cannot recover. A small part of the brain – that part responsible for physical reflexes such as breathing, eye movement, response to pain, swallowing and gagging – remains intact, however, and this can sometimes give the impression that the patient is conscious and responsive.

These high profile cases created enormous controversy and polarization. Many bishops and dioceses issued statements on the matter. In 1991 the Bishops of Washington and Oregon outlined the disputed state of the question as follows:

> On the one hand there are those who maintain that a permanently unconscious person who is sustained by artificially administered nutrition and hydration and is not dying from some other disease or trauma should continue to be nourished. Such nourishment is seen as part of the normal care given to any human being. Furthermore, these people would say that withdrawing artificial nutrition and hydration causes the person's death by omission and can be equivalent to euthanasia. On the other hand, there are those who insist that provision of artificial nutrition and hydration is not obligatory when the burdens clearly outweigh the benefits, and they believe this to be the case when a person has been medically diagnosed as permanently unconscious. They contend that it is an acceptable moral position to view artificially administered hydration and nutrition as a life sustaining treatment like a respirator or dialysis machine. The use of burden/benefit proportionality would indicate it is futile or burdensome or beneficial.

Those who favored allowing the removal of feeding tubes in certified cases of persistent vegetative state, agreed that while some benefit accrues to the patient who is maintained on a feeding tube (i.e., the patient is kept alive), the treatment is futile *in view of the purpose for which we were created* – to know God and love God, to be part of human community, to grow, develop and enjoy life. It maintains physical life, but it will never restore the person to a state enabling him or her to experience life and the grace mediated through it. In these cases, a choice to remove artificial feeding and hydration is not an act of despair or euthanasia, but an admission that the patient's illness is so severe that it makes "achievement of the purpose of life" virtually impossible, and that in an act of trust, we turn that patient's life and salvation over to God. It is also important to remember that in some cases there are side effects of artificial delivery of hydration and nutrition that may make it inadvisable from a medical standpoint.

After a great deal of public debate, especially in the United States where medical resources allow the long-term maintenance of seriously ill patients who are not dying, the Holy See, though its Congregation for the Doctrine of the Faith, issued a clarification in 2007. This statement, "Responses to Certain Question of the United States Conference of Catholic Bishops Concerning Artificial Nutrition and Hydration," made it clear that "in principle" the administration of food and water, by artificial means is an "ordinary and proportionate means of preserving life," even if the patient is deemed to be in a "permanent vegetative state."

It is important to note here that this choice to withdraw any treatment, which is done regretfully, is clearly distinct from a choice of euthanasia, in which the death of the patient is directly willed. Nor is saying that one *may* make such a choice the same as saying that one *must* make such a choice. When we do so, we do so out of faith and hope rather than despair.

Does Appropriate Health Care Change with Age?

Another difficult question is whether the character of health care should change as we grow older. We have all seen statistics about the large percentage of health care dollars which are expended on patients in the last few months or even weeks of their lives. Is there not a point at which we should begin asking, "How much health care is too much?" Advance directives and durable powers of attorney help, but as Christians we need to reshape our overall spiritual presuppositions about life. Sometimes grasping life too tightly can be a spiritual disease.

Daniel Callahan, a noted health care ethicist, has proposed that we begin to think of this in terns of "biographical age." Is there a point, he asks, when our natural life is pretty much drawing to a close, even though we may be in relatively good health? Is there a point when our attitude should shift away from life-prolonging technology and toward the gracious acceptance of death? He writes:

> There are large and growing numbers of elderly who are not imminently dying, but who are feeble and declining, for whom curative medicine has little to offer... For many, old age is a reason in itself to think about medical care in a different way, whether in foregoing its lifesaving powers when death is clearly imminent, or in forgoing its use even when death may be distant but life has become a blight rather than a blessing.[12]

He cites the heavy bias of the Medicare program toward saving and extending life and away from primary care, comfort and palliation. In some cases, the bias toward high-technology life-saving measures is so strong that it's only with difficulty that one can enforce choices for comfort and pain relief only. Norman Paradis writes of such a case in the treatment of his own father:

> When I finally got my father's physicians on the phone, I insisted that he be cared for only by internists who had no incentive to do anything but make him comfortable. Yet my father had been in the hospital two weeks and had spent most of that time receiving "billable" high tech therapy that could not possibly cure him or relieve his pain. We had to forbid them to do anything that was not directly related to relieving his pain.[13]

Callahan believes such cases could be avoided if we allow the elderly to choose their own balance between high-technology curative medicine and low technology care and social support. It is important that we learn to invite the sick and dying to reflect on the meaning of death and to ask them, "How would you like to die?"

The rise of average life expectancy alone has placed tremendous pressure on Medicare, which in 2010 spent nearly a quarter of all its funds on 5% of beneficiaries in their last 12 months of life. While medical advances have been a great blessing to us, they are forcing us to make very difficult decisions about how to divide our national resources various basic goods such as education, defense, and health care. We often treat patients only on the basis of clinical judgments, that is, we ask, "is there a chance this treatment will work?"

We have already shown how the patient's age and condition are important considerations in health care choices. We must be more attentive to subjective factors in making health care choices. Some treatments are too expensive, too burdensome and offer too little promise of benefit to patients who are compromised by age or chronic diseases like diabetes, kidney failure, or heart problems. It is not always a question of less treatment for these patients, but of appropriate treatment that will help them live out their remaining time as actively and happily as possible.

Asceticism and Health Care Choices

The spiritual dimension of such choices is related to asceticism. Philip Keane speaks about the importance of cultivating asceticism as we make our health care choices:

When talking about asceticism we need to be careful not to glorify suffering so that we end up embracing some sort of spiritual masochism. But the ascetic tradition [does] tell us that we need to grasp life lightly, that we sometimes need to be willing to let go of our own personal interests and priorities for the sake of higher values and for the sake of other people...[14]

It is important that we carefully distinguish the consideration of age as a factor in deciding what kind of care is appropriate from proposals for euthanasia or assisted suicide. Allowing people to choose the way in which their final illnesses will be managed is ethically quite distinct from neglecting them, killing them, or helping them kill themselves.

Despite the importance of our bodies and the care which keeps them healthy, physical life is not an absolute value nor an end in itself. The old Baltimore Catechism taught generations of Catholics that God created us to "know him, love him and serve him in this world, and be with him forever in heaven." It is that final union with God which is our real goal in life. So while we should take every reasonable step to assure our good health there are times when Christians must face the fact of mortality and gracefully accept the reality of terminal illness or death. This is why it is inappropriate for Christians to want "everything possible" in health care. There are times when what is possible is not reasonable, given the unlikelihood of success. Health care should enhance life, but it should not deny the reality of death. When health care becomes too aggressive, it not only does not help us spiritually, but can actually be an obstacle to our hope in the resurrection.

Making good health care choices at the end of life requires a certain asceticism, the willingness to forego a good thing for a higher purpose. Instead of seeking every possible treatment the time comes for many of us when we decide that it is time to prepare for death. This should not be a morbid choice, but one filled with joy. As health care ethicists Benedict Ashley and Kevin O'Rourke have said,

> Dying with Christ is an adventure. It is a consequence of, but it need not be a condemnation for, sin. This is a new approach to death, yet it is thoroughly in keeping with the Christian tradition. Indeed, this view of death seems to describe more clearly the experience of Christ, who offered his life rather than have it taken from him, who completed his love and generosity in the final act of obedience to the Father.

Palliative Care, Hospice and the "Happy Death"

Palliative and hospice care are relatively new and still gaining acceptance, but they both represent important advances in care that focus on quality of life and help patients prepare for death. Hospice care provides custom-designed care for those who have a terminal illness and are expected to die within six months. Unfortunately, both patients and physicians sometimes see hospice as a sign of failure or "giving up," so most dying patients enter hospice far too late – sometimes only days before death – for it to have much effect.

Palliative care is not for the dying, but for those who have chronic, incurable diseases that can be managed in a way that gives patients the opportunity to live as comfortably as possible. Both palliative care and hospice make maximize patient control over care and make spirituality an explicit part of the program so that patients can prepare for what we used to call "the happy death" – a death as free from pain and anxiety as possible and anticipated in hope rather than fear.

Philippe Aries describes the difference between this happy, or "tame" death "which was tolerable and familiar, affirmative of the bonds of community and social solidarity, expected with certainty and accepted without crippling fear," and the and the "wild" death, "marked by undue fear and uncertainty, by the presence of medical powers not quite within our mastery, by a course of decline that may leave us isolated and degraded. It is wild because it is alien, because modern technologies make its course highly uncertain, and because it seems removed from a full, fitting presence in the life of the community."

This tame or happy death is the kind we should prepare for. We begin by letting go of little things, trusting that God will continue to give us what we need. Eventually as we age, we let go of – or lose – bigger things, but we still trust that we are moving toward God. When we begin to experience diminishment, we should think about how we want to die, and make our wishes known to those who are likely to be our decision makers.

We abandoned the traditional prayers for a happy death as medical science began to advance, perhaps because we thought we could avoid death altogether. There are many versions of this prayer. Reciting one of them might help us prepare for a happy death:

O God, great and omnipotent judge of the living and the dead, we are to appear before you after this short life to render an account of our works. Give us the grace to prepare for our last hour by a devout and holy life, and protect us against a sudden and unprovided death. Let us remember our frailty and mortality, that we may always live in the ways of your commandments. Teach us to "watch and pray" (Lk 21:36), that when your summons comes for our departure from this world, we may go forth to meet you, experience a merciful judgment, and rejoice in everlasting happiness. We ask this through Christ our Lord. Amen.

An essay this short runs the risk of oversimplifying the complexity of medical ethical decisions. But the areas we have discussed above provide at least the very basic outlines of how to approach such questions. Enhancing patient knowledge and freedom, consulting with family and knowledgeable experts, and remembering that we were not created just to live out our physical lives, but to share God's presence for all eternity are all important ingredients in good choices in medical care.

Chapter 11 – Morality and Public Life: Political Choices in a Diverse Society

A quick glance at the history books shows that for most of the last two thousand years, religious and civil authority were one and the same. Popes crowned emperors, and even had armies that waged fierce battles against kings and princes. There was no such thing as a distinctively civil government that did not have its roots in a divine order presided over by bishops, priests and monks.

All that changed dramatically at the end of the 18th century. Suddenly a half-century of revolutions rudely challenged the church's political prerogatives, displacing religious authority with a new kind of civil authority that had no direct links to the church and that functioned by virtue of reason rather than revelation or religion. Royal families were put to death, churches and monasteries were seized or destroyed by the government and many priests and religious were forced into exile. At about the same time, the thirteen original colonies of the United States were coalescing into a nation – and they did so in a radically new way. The framers of the American constitution declared that the state was to establish no religion as "official". All would be free to practice their religious beliefs as they wished. The American experiment sundered the connection between religious and civil authority once and for all and set the church entirely on its own.

In many ways, this was a great blessing to the church. Now forced to fend for itself and unable to rely upon state support, it would grow quickly and become strong and self-sufficient. But despite the wishes of the founding fathers, America remained deeply religious and there were many bitter disputes about just how religion was to find a home in an officially non-religious country. Today, this tension finds expression in disputes about various schemes for public support of private schools, debates about whether school prayer should be tolerated or even sponsored by government, and pressure to present biblical accounts of creation on an equal footing with evolutionary theories.

Although few Catholics have difficulty reconciling the scientific theory of evolution with Biblical accounts of creation, there are many other areas in which our moral beliefs seem to be compromised by public laws and policies. Federal or state laws on abortion, AIDS information, civil rights for homosexuals, religious education in public schools and a host of other issues pose serious dilemmas for Catholics. How can we support laws which violate our basic moral convictions? Shouldn't the laws we enact reflect the moral truths we know to be true? Sometimes it seems as though the only two alternatives available to us are withdrawal from a sinful society, or imposition of our convictions on a nation. A number of important distinctions might help clarify this thorny question.

Morality and Religion

The first thing we need to remember as we enter these debates is that morality and religion are not necessarily the same thing. There are many moral traditions, including the Roman Catholic one, that begin with a reasoned understanding of the human person rather than with revelation or Scripture. This view of the person, enlightened and clarified by our faith, becomes the basis for deciding what is moral and what is not. Most of the difficult social questions we face today – abortion, civil rights, medical ethics – and cannot be decided purely on the basis of our religious faith. In many instances the Bible has nothing at all to say on these topics, so we are left to our intelligence and reason to discover answers. While we sometimes equate "moral" with "religious" in fact there is a more basic moral code, one that we might call "common human morality", that all reasonable people can seek and understand. In a pluralistic society, it is this common moral base, and not the imposition of religious views, that we must seek.

In the abortion debate, for example, opponents of abortion rightly argue from a pro-life stance. Yet their arguments often appeal to the words of Scripture and make it seem as though *only religious believers* can understand these arguments. Pro-choice activists reject these arguments as "merely religious" and say that they have no place in a society where there is no established religion. "I do not share your religious faith," they say, "therefore your arguments in favor of the God-given sanctity of life are not convincing to me." Abortion is surely a moral issue, but it is not necessarily a religious issue. Anybody who understands what human life is – and one does not need religious faith to do that – can understand why abortion might be wrong. Political candidates who state that they are "opposed to abortion on the basis of their religious belief, but do not want to impose that belief on others" are placing abortion in a strictly religious category which makes it easy to reject. In a pluralistic society our task is not to impose our views on others, but to try to convince others of our deeply held convictions by cogent, well-reasoned arguments.

Morality and Public Policy

The second important distinction is between morality and public policy. *Morality* (and this includes both religious morality and "common sense" morality) is geared to personal perfection. It is internal, intentional and deeply personal. Like charm or character or honesty, it cannot be forced upon someone but must flow from within. In this sense, it is true to say that "morality cannot be legislated" – it can only be freely assumed by people who have chosen it because of its evident beauty.

Public policy or civil law, on the other hand, has a much more modest goal. Unlike morality, which aims at the inner perfection of persons, laws and public policies aim primarily at public order. For this reason, laws that regulate drinking, banking or the sale of guns do not *make* people moral, but create the relatively harmonious and peaceful environment in which we are able to pursue morality. Few of us, for example, would be able to cultivate the virtues of truth, prudence, temperance or patience if we lived in a society which was torn by strife and insurrection. Public policy tries to achieve the minimum necessary for all of us to live together in peace. It tries to protect us from danger, provide basic goods like housing, education, medical care and employment, and regulate the distribution of commodities like electricity, fuel and food. These things are all vitally necessary and enable us to seek morality, but they are not the same thing as morality.

The truth of this distinction is evident if we think for a moment about things which are *moral but not legal*: it may not be a sin to exceed the speed limit, drink alcohol after 2:00 a.m., park in a no-parking zone or refuse to report for military duty; but each of these are usually seen as violations of the law and will be punished as such. There are also things which are *legal but not moral:* sex with someone other than your spouse, "bending" laws to limit employee wages, drinking to excess, lust, and so forth. And of course, there are things which may be both illegal and immoral: cheating, bribery, lying, killing. The important thing to note here is that there is not a perfect correspondence between civil laws, which govern our life together and create a harmonious social context, and morality, which governs our personal lives and makes us good persons. The two are not unrelated, but they are not exactly the same, either. Confusing them often results in disaster, as did the unfortunate attempt to prohibit the consumption of alcohol in this country in the 1920s. Not only did prohibition not create a nation of temperate men and women, it created widespread disregard for the law and may well have given birth to organized crime, which plagues us to this day. Laws that try to enforce morality or which do not have adequate support from the community on which they are imposed are bad laws and are doomed to failure.

The abortion issue is one of those cases today where morality and public policy do not always intersect. While many people feel abortion is immoral because it is murder, many others feel just as strongly that it is not murder, and should be placed in another category. The problem sis that there is a fundamental disagreement about what kind of act abortion is. Is it a noble act of free choice, or the deliberate taking of human life? Until now, at least, this fundamental disagreement has made consensus on abortion impossible.

The big challenge is that there is no social consensus on the moral status of the early embryo. Is it a person, a pre-person, or something else? This is the most important question, and yet neither pro-life nor pro-choice advocates are willing to discuss it for fear of losing ground.

Although we may be convinced that the embryo is a person from the moment of conception and that abortion is therefore seriously immoral, many other people of good will would disagree with us. This does not mean that we should water down our own convictions. But we must remember good law – which is always oriented to public order – must be feasible; that is, it must have the support of a significant portion of the populace before it can be enacted. While abortion may indeed be immoral, it is not clear that sufficient public consensus exists today to eliminate abortion by legislation. Consequently, we will have to find other strategies to reduce or eliminate abortion. Doing so does not mean we are "soft on abortion," but that we are realistic about what legislation can and cannot accomplish. Simply declaring that human life exists at a certain point, or making abortion illegal on that basis will not stop abortion unless a significant proportion of the population agrees with those presuppositions.

Politics and the Gospel of Life

In his 1995 encyclical, *The Gospel of Life (Evangelium Vitae)* Pope John Paul II offers a detailed analysis of cultural trends which threaten life. The issues he treats – abortion, embryo experimentation, euthanasia, suicide and capital punishment – are all moral issues, but they have important implications for civil law, as well. This makes the encyclical of interest to legislators and citizens alike.

The Pope begins with the biblical story of Cain, who in the fourth chapter of Genesis killed his brother Abel out of jealousy. When God asks Cain what he has done, Cain asks, "Am I my brother's keeper?" Just as Cain "does not wish to think about his brother and refuses to accept the responsibility which every person has towards others, so in our own society this trend is manifest in an emerging "culture of death," in which "broad sectors of public opinion justify certain crimes against life in the name of rights of individual freedom, and on this basis they claim not only exemption from punishment but even authorization by the state..."(#4). The Pope sees symptoms of this disregard for life in lack of solidarity with "society's weakest members – such as the elderly, the infirm, immigrants, children and the indifference frequently found in relations between the world's peoples even when basic values such as survival, freedom and peace are involved." (#8)

The Pope lists several factors which have brought this cultural situation about: a profound *crisis of culture*, which generates skepticism in relation to the very foundations of knowledge and ethics, and which makes it increasingly difficult to grasp clearly the meaning of what man is, the meaning of his rights and duties. Then there are all kinds of *existential and interpersonal difficulties,* made worse by the complexity of a society in which individuals, couples and families are often left alone with their problems. Finally, there are *situations of acute poverty, anxiety or frustration* in which the struggle to make ends meet, the presence of unbearable pain, or instances of violence, especially against women" all of which "make the choice to defend and promote life so demanding as sometimes to reach the point of heroism." (#11)

The roots of this problem lie in an extreme subjectivity, which "recognizes as a subject of rights only the person who enjoys full or at least incipient autonomy and who emerges from a state of total dependence on others." This in turn heightens individual freedom so much that any notion of life in society is distorted, and there is no place for "solidarity, openness to others and service of them..." Eventually, everyone is considered an enemy from whom one has to defend oneself. Society becomes a mass of individuals placed side by side, but without any mutual bonds." (#19,20)

The Pope suggests that commitment to the Gospel of Life, which "includes everything that human experience and reason tell us about the value of human life, accepting it, purifying it, exalting it and bringing it to fulfillment" (#30), will remedy this sad trend. He specifically addresses a number of human life issues which are currently under consideration by legislative bodies around the world.

Capital Punishment (#55-56)

Although he stresses the inviolability of the command "Do not kill," the Pope admits that there are some cases, analogous to self-defense, in which "the right to protect one's own life and the duty not to harm someone else's life are difficult to reconcile in practice." While it is never legitimate to take the life of an innocent person, the Pope says that because governments have a right and duty to protect the lives of their citizens, there may be cases in which a criminal poses such a grave threat to a society that only taking his life will provide safety to citizens. Punishments for crimes ought to "fulfill the purpose of defending public order and ensuring people's safety, while at the same time offering the offender an incentive to help to change his or her behavior and be rehabilitated." He allows that in very rare circumstances, execution may be necessary, but only "when it would not be possible otherwise to defend society. Today however, such cases are very rare, if not practically non-existent."

The Pope's view is dependent on seeing society as a whole, as a kind of organism or body which sometimes has diseased or dysfunctional parts that must be removed for the good of the whole. Viewed from this perspective, the death penalty should not be seen as retribution, but as a regrettable necessity, invoked only when the criminal poses a direct threat to society. Except in emergencies or wartime, it is difficult to imagine circumstances in which execution is the only possible way of eliminating the threat that a criminal poses to public safety.

Abortion and Embryonic Experimentation (#58-63)

The most difficult moral questions we face today revolve around the rights of unborn children. As I already pointed out, the problem is rooted in controversy about the status of the embryo. Many members of our society will not acknowledge the full personhood of the embryo and will not grant it protection of the law.

The Pope acknowledges the centuries-long controversy about the exact moment at which the embryo is "ensouled," and becomes a human person. He admits that there is no scientific way to demonstrate when this occurs, but says that if the existence of a human person is probable, it should be protected:

> Even if the presence of a spiritual soul cannot be ascertained by empirical data, the results themselves of scientific research on the human embryo provide a valuable indication for discerning by the use of reason a personal presence at the moment of the first appearance of a human life: how could a human individual not be a human person?...the mere probability that a human person is involved would suffice to justify an absolutely clear prohibition of any intervention aimed at killing a human embryo. (#60)

In doubtful cases like these, it is useful to recall an example which was used by moral theologians for centuries. They cited the case of a hunter in the woods who saw movement among the trees. A glimpse was not enough to determine whether the movement was caused by a person or a deer. Should he go ahead and shoot anyway, hoping to hit a deer? Moral theologians always held that in such cases, where there was even possibly a person, the prudent hunter would refrain. The Pope's argument about abortion is similar. Even if the biological or genetic "glimpse" we have of the embryo cannot prove definitively that the embryo is ensouled from the moment of conception, it is certainly possible, and even probable, that it is. Rather than risk the deliberate killing of an innocent child, we should rule out abortion in every case.

The same argument applies to embryonic research that is not directed to healing or that involves disproportionate risks or side effects to the embryo. Just as we would not use adults as objects of experimentation (the horrible experiments of Nazi doctors on living subjects comes to mind), so too if embryos are, or even might be, full persons, we must not objectify them by making them "matter" for experiments which are of no benefit to them.

An even more drastic case involves deliberately bringing an embryo into existence for the express purpose of experimentation or therapy for another person. A television hospital drama once related the case of a man who was suffering from rapidly advancing Parkinson's disease, which causes progressive damage to the nervous system. Because there is some evidence that fetal brain tissue may halt or reverse the damage caused by the disease, he and his wife agreed to get pregnant in order to create an embryo whose brain tissue could then be harvested and used therapeutically to halt the progress of his disease. Their plans were a clear violation of the dignity of that embryo, as the Pope says clearly when he speaks of procedures that exploit living human embryos and fetuses, sometimes specifically "produced" for this purpose by *in vitro* fertilization – either to be used as "biological material" or as providers of organs or tissue for transplants in the treatment of certain diseases. The killing of innocent human creatures, even if carried out to help others, constitutes an absolutely unacceptable act. (#63)

Suicide and Euthanasia (#64-67)

The third threat which the Pope sees to the Gospel of Life is a tendency in our prosperous and efficient societies to see the "growing number of elderly and disabled people as intolerable and burdensome." (#64) This may lead us to consider euthanasia, which by omission or commission, involves an intention to "take control of death and bring it about before its time." The Pope carefully distinguishes these intentional acts of killing from choices to forego futile or aggressive treatments which offer little hope to the patient. Even painkillers which may hasten death are permissible as long as the intent is only to relieve pain and is in no way to cause the patient's death. Patients may choose, of course, to accept some pain in order to "share consciously in the Lord's passion," but the Pope considers such a choice heroic and not the duty of everyone. Repeating the teaching of Pope Pius XII, Pope John Paul II notes that the use of painkillers is licit, even if they shorten life, as long as "death is not willed or sought, even though for reasonable motives one runs the risk of it." (#65)

The culture of death can also make suicide seem like an honorable choice, especially in old age or in the face of serious, progressive illness. But *Evangelium Vitae* insists that suicide remains a "grave evil," which "involves the rejection of love of self and the renunciation of the obligation of justice and charity towards one's neighbor, towards the communities to which one belongs and towards society as a whole. In its deepest reality, suicide represents a rejection of God's absolute sovereignty over life and death..." (#66).

Dr. Jack Kevorkian became notorious for his promotion of assisted suicide, helping another to complete an act of self-destruction. This, the Pope says, "is false mercy." True compassion does not lead us to help each other end our lives, but to "sharing another's pain. Assisted suicide and euthanasia are acts of betrayal which violate justice and mutual trust, "which are the basis of every authentic interpersonal relationship of life."

Our belief in the Resurrection draws us to resist such solutions to suffering and death. They cry of those who are faced with the "temptation to give up in utter desperation" is not a cry for destruction, but rather "a request for companionship, sympathy and support in the time of trial. It is a plea for help to keep on hoping when all human hopes fail." (#67).

These arguments sound strange to our ears, which have been conditioned by materialism to believe that the human spirit is overwhelmed by pain and deprivation, and by individualism, which denies the reality of our human relationships. If we believe we are totally autonomous individuals, completely separate from others , then the choice to take our lives, or to ask another to help us end our lives is entirely personal and private. But if we see ourselves as incomplete without the friendships and love of those around us, if we believe that those relationships constitute us and make us fully human, then the choice to take our own lives is indeed an injustice to those friends who actually "own" a part of us. Asking someone else for help in self-destruction is an insult to their love for us.

The importance of pastoral care for the sick and dying and for their loved ones is obvious. At these moments, our hope and faith are stretched thin and we are in special need of the solace, encouragement and prayers of others. Chaplains and priests must take their responsibility here very seriously, shepherding the dying and their families through the valley of death to a clear vision of God's promise of eternal life.

How Should Catholics Vote?

After outlining these threats to the dignity of life, the Pope turns to the responsibilities of citizens and politicians in protecting life. He notes that there should be a "continuity" between moral law and civil law, since both are rooted in reason and objective truth and that public laws can never be solely a matter of achieving the will of the majority. (#70-72) But he also notes that civil law is more narrow in scope than morality, since its purpose is "to guarantee an ordered social coexistence in true justice, so that all may lead a quiet and peaceable life, godly and respectful in every way." (#71)

Laws which legitimize abortion, suicide or euthanasia in any way are inherently unjust and are in complete opposition to the right to life proper to every person. Willing participation in the passage or execution of such laws or participation in the intention of those who do, involves direct cooperation with evil and is never permitted. This means that conscientious citizens may never obey such a law, or "take part in a propaganda campaign in favor of such a law, or vote for it." (#73) Similarly, medical care personnel must refuse direct participation in such "acts against life," and may have to sacrifice their professional positions if they are compelled to participate.

The Pope acknowledges that legislators sometimes find themselves in the very difficult position of knowing that they cannot defeat a law which permits abortion or euthanasia; their only choices may be to leave the permissive law as it is, or vote for a measure which reduces, but does not eliminate, the threat to life. In these cases, "when it is not possible to overturn or completely abrogate a pro-abortion law, an elected official whose absolute personal opposition to procured abortion was well known, could licitly support proposals aimed at limiting the harm done by such a law and at lessening its negative consequences..." (#73). In such a case, the legislator is not cooperating with the evil of such a law, but doing her best to limit its evil aspects.

The Pope refers here to the principle of toleration, which means that we must sometimes settle for less-than-perfect laws that preserve public order but do not eliminate all sinful acts. He refers to a famous passage in the *Summa Theologica* of St. Thomas Aquinas, in which Aquinas asks "Whether it belongs to civil law to repress all vice?"[15] Thomas notes that civil laws do indeed allow some vices, or sins, because "human law is framed for a number of human beings, the majority of whom are not perfect in virtue. Wherefore human laws do not forbid all vices, from which only the virtuous abstain, but only the more grievous vices, from which it is possible for the majority to abstain."

He makes a similar point in reference to the rites of unbelievers, which in the time of St. Thomas Aquinas were clearly seen as sinful. The practice of these rites should be tolerated by law, Thomas says, because to try to repress them might result in war or civil strife. This would undermine the overall purpose of law, which is to preserve public order. In making his argument, Thomas drew on the earlier experience of St. Augustine with the legal toleration of prostitution. While Augustine admitted that prostitution flowed from lust and was morally wrong, he argued that we could not eradicate it by law, and that trying to do so would result in a worse situation in which "society was convulsed by lust." Though far from a perfect solution, he said, we should be content to limit prostitution as much as possible and thus preserve public order.[16]

The parallel with abortion is this: even though many people recognize abortion as killing of the innocent, and therefore morally wrong, we may have to tolerate laws which allow some abortions because many members of society do not share our views and would not obey more restrictive laws. Trying to make abortion illegal would not eliminate abortion and would also result in an industry of illegal abortions which would undermine the overall purpose of law. So in some cases, the best we may be able to do is gradually reduce the number of abortions by a number of means, legislative and social, while tolerating them legally, though by no means approving of them, in the meantime. This involves cultivation of political patience on our part as we realize that moral perfection and political peace is achieved gradually and over a long period of time.

Voting for the Common Good

When Catholics go to the polls, they should remember first of all that a moral consensus among Christians, Jews, Muslims and non-believers is possible – but that it is an elusive reality and is achieved only with dialogue and patience. As we prepare to vote, we should listen to different moral opinions carefully, sifting them for what is truly human and valid. The goal of our political life is not to impose the superiority of one religious view over another, but to find a kind of compromise which will enable us all to live in peace. This will not make us moral. But it will provide the environment in which we are able to pursue morality and train our children in it. At times, public policy will seem painfully thin or even deficient. But we must remember that it is not an end in itself but only a precondition for the real purpose of our lives.

Our voting should also involve a careful analysis of all the positions a candidate offers. It will be rare that we find one candidate who supports every value we hold, but we should always try to find the best combination. The key here is *the common good*. Which candidate offers the best hope, overall, of providing for all the things we need in common: education, economic stability, protection of life, medical care, public safety, or defense? Selecting a candidate on the basis of his or her views on only one topic is almost always a mistake. No single value, no matter how important, is an adequate guide for the complex task of government, which exists in order to make our life in common and the pursuit of our individual goals possible.

"You Did It To Me: A New Culture of Human Life"

Perhaps the most important part of *Evangelium Vitae* is the last section, in which the Pope describes how the promotion of a "culture of life" is everyone's responsibility. Although he focuses on the importance of good legislation and the role of faith in preserving human life from the dignity of abortion, suicide, euthanasia and capital punishment, in this last section he emphasizes that the Gospel of Life is not for believers alone, because "life has a sacred and religious value that every human being can grasp by the light of reason."(#101) It is the whole of human society which must work for the common good by acknowledging and defending the right to life.

Christians are people who have been sent to preach the Gospel of Life, and we have a responsibility not just to limit the influence of evil, but to "celebrate life with our whole existence, and to serve it with the programs and structures which support and promote life." (#79). In the final section of *Evangelium Vitae*, Pope John Paul II describes duties which fall to many different classes of persons in preaching this Gospel and promoting the beauty and dignity of human life.

He addresses first teachers, catechists and theologians, who must illustrate the "anthropological reasons" upon which respect for human life is based. It is their duty to show what human life is, and how our choices can protect it. They are also responsible for the formation of conscience and the cultivation of liturgical and private prayer, enriched by the symbols and gestures of our own tradition and those from other cultures and peoples. Such prayer fosters contemplation and draws us into a community which rejoices in the gift of life. *Daily living* is part of our spiritual worship when it is filled with praise, gratitude and generosity. This daily should include "gestures of sharing" such as organ donation.

We must also encourage vocations to service which will help promote marriage and responsible procreation. Social service agencies can help meet the challenges of hardship by providing care for those afflicted with drug addition, mental illness, and AIDS as well as those who struggle with disabilities or the infirmities of old age. Hospitals, clinics and convalescent homes should be places in which "suffering, pain and death are acknowledged and understood in their human and specifically Christian meaning." Such institutions should be staffed by health care personnel and administrators who serve as "guardians and servants of human life."

The role of civil leaders is crucial too. They are called to make good choices for the common good, but always bearing in mind what is realistically attainable. (#90) But the importance of civil leadership should not overshadow the importance of maximum "participation in social and political life" (#93) by all citizens. This is especially important at a time in which political participation is declining because so many citizens have become cynical or apathetic about the role of government. Government need not be seen only as a necessary evil, but as a means of distributing social goods and organizing human effort in a constructive way. Indeed, in a very enlightening passage which refutes the notion that government is an evil or merely a means of restraining our sinful impulses, St. Thomas Aquinas affirms that government would even have existed in paradise. This is so, he says, because humans are naturally social, and even before sin some means would have been necessary to organize life toward the common good.[17] This means that our common life is something for which all of us have a responsibility, not just politicians or government.

Intellectuals have a duty to "offer serious and well documented contributions" which promote life. Those who work in the mass media need "to present noble models of life and make room for instances of people's positive and sometimes heroic love for one another."

He assigns a primary role to the family, or "domestic church." The responsibility of the family begins with responsible procreation and raising children. "By word and example, in the daily round of relations and choices, and through concrete actions and signs, parents lead their children to authentic freedom, actualized in the sincere gift of self. [Their role] also includes teaching and giving their children an example of the true meaning of suffering and death and...fostering attitudes of closeness, assistance and sharing towards sick or elderly members of the family." (#92)

Evangelium Vitae singles out the elderly who must in some way always remain a part of the family, by re-establishing a kind of "covenant" between the generations. While they must be the special object of our concern, they must also be valued for the contribution they make to the Gospel of Life through "the rich treasury of experiences they have acquired" which make them "sources of wisdom and witnesses of hope and love." (#94)

Pope John Paul's message calls for a "general mobilization of consciences" in order to activate a great campaign in support of life. He calls first of all for the renewal of individual hearts, then of the church itself, the communion of believers, then of political and social life, which will help us protect and promote human life wherever it is threatened. He urges us to work in all of these arenas to uncover the brilliant image of God which is planted deep within our lives together, but which has been tarnished by neglect and the narrow pursuit of individual goods.

Chapter 12 – Sexual Morality:
Wholeness and Holiness

When he wrote his great *Summa Theologiae* 750 years ago, St. Thomas Aquinas made an astonishing statement: "Sex is to the human race," he said, "what food is to the body." This is a startling assertion because it shows a profound awareness of the centrality of sex to human life – as basic as food itself. Even more importantly it suggests that far from being a private act which is done between "consenting adults," as we say today, sex is a highly social reality. Although he does speak of the sexual act as expressive of love and as a sign of marital fidelity, for him the most important thing about sex is that it perpetuates humankind and thus has important social implications.

Why Do People Have Sex?

The fundamental question in sexual morality is "Why do people have sexual intercourse?" The reasons vary, and depending on whether they contribute to human fulfillment or not, they are judged to be either moral or immoral. Most of us would agree that having sex to express love and affection for one's spouse, to start a family, or to renew marital fidelity are good (i.e., "moral") reasons to have sex. Using sex as a commodity, as a means to something else (money, prestige, status, security) would be repellent to us; we would see it as literally "selling ourselves." Having sex just for the fun of it, even with people we do not know well is widely accepted in our culture today, but we would have to agree that such sexual activity falls far short of the kind of intimacy and self-sharing of which sex is capable. And engaging in sex out of vengeance or anger (as in the case of rape) is not only immoral but criminal as well.

Through most of history one reason for sex – procreation – outweighed all the others. In St. Thomas' day, for example, the high infant mortality rate forced women to remain pregnant through the majority of their childbearing years. Some women were pregnant 15 or 20 times during their lives in order to see six or eight children survive. Procreation was of crucial importance because children were security. In an age when there were no retirement plans or social security and the accumulation of wealth was very difficult, a large family was one's only guarantee of economic security. Until recent times it was virtually impossible to live as a single person. One had to have a family – whether a natural one or the adopted family of a monastery or convent – in order to survive. For the vast majority of the population, there were no real alternatives.

Social conditions in the 20th century are very different. We are able to put money in the bank, invest in retirement plans and be assured of social security. Remaining single poses no economic problem. Childlessness, while often regrettable, is no longer the stigma it once was. In fact, couples today can choose to remain childless or to plan their families according to financial or other needs. Since our infant mortality rate is lower today, and since our economy is structured in such a way that large numbers of offspring are no longer necessary for economic security, people have as many children as they want (often no more than two or three). When they pass the age of childbearing, the purpose of sexual intercourse focuses more directly on expression of love, shaping of individual character, bonding as a couple, "speaking" one's personality or affection. Church teaching has reflected this shift. For centuries church documents spoke of the "primary" and "secondary" purposes of sex (procreation and mutual love, respectively). The most recent documents do not distinguish them and see procreation and mutual love as equally important.

While people obviously do have sex in order to procreate, that is not the only reason they do so. Other reasons for having sex – what theologian Frank Nichols has calls the "surplus value" of intercourse – have taken on a greater importance in our own age.[18] Nichols says that after the procreative aspect of sex has been realized, (which often occurs today by the time people are in their forties, when they have had as many children as they can provide for economically) people still continue to have sex, but for different reasons. At this point, the meaning of sexuality moves away from procreation and begins to focus on other values. Nichols says that at this point in life, sex should be *totalizing*, so that it involves our whole persons and allows total self-giving; it should be *plastic* – "not in the sense of artificial, but in the sense of moldable, in such a way that it helps shape us into whole persons; it should also be *other-directed, life-giving,* and have rich *sign value.* It should always point beyond itself to the commitment and generativity it signifies.

Sex as Language

These qualities suggest that sex is not just a means to the end of procreation, but a language, a way of "speaking ourselves," or a kind of self-communication. Like any other kind of language, sexual language can be spoken well or poorly, tenderly or abusively, honestly or dishonestly, lovingly or manipulatively. Sex can be the violent language of rape, the consumerist language of prostitution, the affirming language of loving marital sex. Like any language, it is learned through imitation and sensory experience. While it continues to develop throughout our lives, the most important years are those of early childhood. As the noted Redemptorist theologian Bernard Häring says:

> Everyone knows that learning languages, including the child's learning of the mother tongue, necessarily entails the right to make mistakes. Dramatizing a learner's grammatical errors or ridiculing a child's mispronunciations inhibits the learning process. There is something similar in sexual development. The sexual language has to be learned gradually and dramatizing the imperfections and mistakes of childhood leads to the alienation of sexuality.[19]

Scientists today tell us that this sexual language begins forming before birth as the brain and our sexual organs are shaped by the prenatal influence of hormones. At birth, some of our basic sexual language has already been determined. There is a "maleness" or "femaleness" programmed into our brains before we are even born.

In the early years of childhood, more specific elements of the sexual language – syntax and grammar, if you will – are shaped by relations with parents, siblings and others. Depending on what these influences are and when they take place, a child's sexual development may be normal and mutual or may become more or less distorted. We know, for example, that a relatively constant percentage of the population is homosexual or bisexual, and that a certain number of others suffer from sexual pathologies which compel them to seek sexual satisfaction with children, or by means of inappropriate dress or behavior (e.g., cross-dressing or stalking), self-inflicted pain, or violence.

In the worst cases, these pathologies become compulsive and criminally destructive. Jeffrey Dahmer and John Wayne Gacy, who were both convicted of mutilating and murdering dozens of young men, are examples of persons whose sexual language was severely deformed. Unable to establish normal, mutual sexual relationships, they could only find satisfaction in sexual activity that was linked to pain and death. These sexual pathologies are virtually impossible to cure because the aberrant desire was impressed deep into the brain at an early age and by a process we do not fully understand. By the time evidence of the desires emerges, it is too late.

Fortunately, such catastrophic failures in the development of a normal sexual language are very rare. But they do remind us that sex is an acquired language, and that parental instruction and example are very important. A good analogy is teaching a child to play a musical instrument or learn a foreign language. Children who are taught with love and patience will likely grow up loving the musical or linguistic skill they have acquired. Those whose learning was traumatic, painful and sprinkled with corporal punishment will probably not only fail to learn to play well, but will hate it besides. Similarly, children who are taught about sex honestly and lovingly, and who see their parents treat each other's bodies and hearts with respect will be much more likely to learn to speak a sexual language that is whole and life giving. Children who are taught to associate sex with fear, danger or punishment will incorporate that into their sexual language and will be limited in their ability love and sustain relationships.

Homosexuality presents a special case, in which a child acquires a variant language of sexual self-expression. Scientists are not sure exactly what "causes" homosexuality, but evidence indicates that it is the result of a complex series of pre-natal and early childhood influences. Most specialists agree that sexual identity, homosexual or otherwise, is largely determined by the age of five or six. Homosexuality does not fall into the same category as the sexual pathologies described above because gay men and women can lead happy and productive lives. Although the Catholic tradition says that sexual activity between persons of the same sex lacks the generativity and complementarity necessary for marriage, church documents stress that all of us – gay or straight – share in the basic dignity God gave us:

> The human person, made in the image and likeness of God, can hardly be adequately described by a reductionist reference to his or her sexual orientation. Everyone living on the face of the earth has personal problems and difficulties, but challenges to growth, strengths, talents and gifts as well.[20]

This suggests that God's image encompasses all sexuality and that holiness can be found in any state of life. Gay and lesbian persons should strive to find this image of God within them, and to realize the values of faithfulness, generativity, self-giving, charity and justice as fully as they can. It is important that they never reduce themselves to their sexual identity in such a way that God's grace and love are excluded. Similarly, parents of gay or lesbian children must discover and affirm their children's gifts and talents, and help them learn how to fulfill the vocation of holiness to which all of us are called.

Sex as Self-Communication

Because sex is not only a means of procreation but a way of intimate self-communication, the church has always insisted that sex should be reserved to the safety and security of a permanent marital relationship. Just as we hesitate to tell much about ourselves to strangers or to people whom we do not trust, so we should not speak our very selves sexually to someone we do not know or to whom we are not committed. Doing so places us in danger of being hurt by misunderstanding or abuse. Speaking a mature and holy sexual language means knowing when and where to speak it; it means knowing that some things can only be said in protected environments and that whenever we "speak ourselves" promiscuously or casually, we are hurting ourselves and limiting the great act of self-sharing which sex is.

Sex as a Sacrament

Those of us who were raised in the pre-Vatican II church remember that a sacrament was defined as "an outward sign instituted by Christ to give grace." We identified those sacraments with the seven specific ritual activities which took place in church or in the confessional. But these specific sacramental moments are rooted in a broader notion of sacramentality which says that God acts through real, tangible things including, but not limited to, bread, wine, water, oil and laying on of hands in order to communicate his presence to us.

This is one of the most distinctive features of Catholic theology. It extends to marriage, where the couple actually effect the sacrament themselves by speaking their marriage vows (which God then "uses" as an occasion of grace). But it goes beyond the church ceremony and continues into the lives of the married couple whose vows only begin to unfold as the marriage ceremony ends. Their whole lives together become sacramental. Each time they express love, or faithfulness or affection, they create an opportunity for grace to enter into their lives. This grace "builds on" the human acts of love and affection. In an even more profound way, the sexual act itself, as the most intimate experience of married life, becomes the supreme sacrament of marriage. As the couple experiences the pleasure, comfort and ecstasy of sexual love, they offer God a vast opportunity to enter into their lives. Philip Keane describes this sacramentality:

> Everything about marriage, including its explicitly sexual aspects is part of the sacrament. Past fear of human sexuality may have been part of the reason why the marriage ceremony, rather than the whole marriage, popped into mind when we spoke about "sacrament." But all the married couple's giving to one another and to their children are part of the sacrament. Sexual intercourse is a major element in the sacramental life of the couple. In this context, it can be understood as a liturgical or worshipful action.[21]

Theologian Denise Lardner Carmody takes this notion further, linking the holiness of sexuality to the Trinity:

> When we make love, the love of Father, Son and Spirit circulate, come into place...Can it be that the Spirit is the kindly light in which we are attractive to one another? Are the excitement, the arousal, the need, the pain we experience relevant to what makes up the life of God?... Human orgasm bespeaks the ecstasy wrought by the divine perfection.[22]

Seen in this way, it is obvious that the fuller the expression of love, the more fully sacramental, i.e., revelatory of God, it is. Conversely, the more restricted and truncated and conditional the sexual act is (such as when it is between two people who hardly know each other or when it is undertaken only for self-gratification) the more the sacramental possibility is diminished or even eliminated. The act is too shallow and barren to even bear its own weight much less the weight of God's grace. Rather than a necessary evil which may actually compromise holiness, marital sex is a means to holiness and grace.

Sex as Generative

Theologians from St. Thomas down to our own day have spoken eloquently about the essentially procreative nature of sexuality. We have seen how that was partly due to economic necessity; children were essential to economic survival. But it also bespoke the need for sex to create something outside of itself. In our own age when lower infant mortality and different economic structures make procreation somewhat less necessary, other reasons, such as the "self-speaking" described above, have emerged as important justifications for sexual intercourse. But even in view of these important developments, one thing remains constant: that sex, in order to be authentic and fully sacramental, must be generative.

Even for couples who cannot or choose not to have children, their marriage and sexual life must continue to generate something outside of itself. The self-speaking and affirmation of the other which takes place in sex is important, of course; but to be like God's own love, which generated all of creation, our love-making must also create and renew. It must first create and renew the partners themselves, enabling them to form a common project which will create and renew those outside of their marriage. In this way, marriage becomes an ongoing sacrament, or sign of God's presence to the world. It is not just a private act between two people, but powerful witness and social force. Fr. Andre Guindon refers to this generative quality as sexual fecundity, which includes, but is not limited to, biological procreation.[23]

The Virtue of Chastity

In an earlier chapter we talked about the virtue of temperance, which has to do with our desires, and which is particularly related to pleasures of touch. Chastity is a part of the virtue of temperance. Although we sometimes think of chastity as having only to do with restraint, in fact it is the virtue which helps us *integrate* our desire for intimacy and sexual pleasure with the rest of our lives. Chastity is not mere abstinence from sex. We may abstain from sex for any number of reasons: fatigue, overwork, fear of punishment, anger. But none of these motives constitutes chastity. The virtue of chastity leads us to forego sex, not because it is bad, nor because we fear punishment, but because we want to use our sexual ability as it should be used, given our goal in life. We cultivate chastity when we choose sex because it will help us be who we want to be.

Chastity does not eliminate our sexual desire; rather, it trains our desires so that they contribute to a full and satisfying human life. The chaste person is one who is not afraid of or terrified or controlled by sexual desire, but who has made desire a normal, healthy part of his or her life. As Ronald Lawler, Joseph Boyle and William May say in their book:

> Chastity is the virtue by which a person "frees love from selfishness and aggression"... It can be more fully described as a virtue concerned with the intelligent and loving integration of our sexual desires and affections into our being as persons, enabling us to come into possession of ourselves as sexual beings so that we can love well – and so that we can touch others and allow ourselves to be touched in ways that fully respect the goods of human existence... Chastity does not seek to suppress or deny sexuality, but rather enables a person to put loving and intelligent order into his passional life, to take possession of his desires so that the whole self can be at peace.[24]

Vigen Guroian,[25] an Orthodox theologian, says that marriage (and sex itself) should be an "icon" – not a mere picture of God, but an actual window on the divine. Can we see sex as such a powerful gift? Can we link our explicitly sexual moments with the great wonder of sacramental life offered to us in Baptism, Eucharist and Reconciliation? If we can, we are taking an important step toward discovering the fullness of life God has in store for us.

Chapter 13 – Vocation and Virtue: The Heart of Ethical Business Practices

The journalist and professional cynic Ambrose Bierce once defined a corporation as "an ingenious device for obtaining individual profit without individual responsibility." Recent business scandals suggest that his definition was accurate. Deceptive accounting practices, insider trading, and massive executive compensation not only led to bankruptcy of several large corporations, but to the loss of jobs and pensions for thousands of employees. These scandals will force us to ask basic questions about the way we do business. They will probably result in new regulatory legislation. But laws are not enough. Because corporations are created by persons who make moral choices, we must also ask how a renewed understanding of vocation and spirituality can reshape business from the inside out.

Where Does Business Go Wrong?

The reasons for these business failures are complex. It will be a long time before we fully understand what happened. However, most experts agree on several things that were important contributing factors. The first is the "bricks vs. clicks" dilemma. With traditional corporations, like General Motors or United Airlines, there is a certain amount of "hard capital" to which a precise value can be assigned. When we invest in these companies, we know that there is inventory, factories or supplies that have a real market value. With the new "dot-com" businesses, however, it is much more difficult to assign a value. How much is an idea worth? How do you assign a precise value to a software code or a network of service providers? Some of the corporations that collapsed had a lot of "intellectual capital" but very little in the way of "bricks," so their value was speculative. As a result, many were overvalued.

Another factor is lack of government oversight. There has been a tendency to deregulate many businesses in recent years. This is based on the hope that less regulation will result in more competition, which will ultimately lead to lower prices and better service for the consumer. Marjorie Kelly, editor of *Business Ethics*, summarizes this argument: "Unregulated markets are ideal. Left free to work its magic, self-interest (e.g., greed) ostensibly leads things to work out for the benefit of all, as though guided by an invisible hand." She notes that unfortunately this does not always happen in practice. Deregulation and free market competition sometimes lead to aggressive practices that wipe out small competitors, or inflate the market and raise prices.

A third factor is the fact that executive compensation was linked to closely to short-term profits. Executives were often given "options," or the right to buy stock at a certain price, even if its market value went up. This encouraged them to make decisions that might help the short term value of the stock, but make the entire corporation unstable in the long run. Lawrence Ellison, CEO of the Oracle Corporation set a record for executive compensation last year by earning $706 million. He did this by selling millions of shares of stock and exercising stock options when things started looking bad. His actions caused the company to lose a third of its value within a month.[26]

Vocation and the "Spirituality of Business"

Despite these discouraging examples, there is hope. Business ethics professor Kenneth Goodpaster sees a growing interest in work, spirituality and ethics. "The buzzwords and phrases are everywhere," he says, "Servant leadership, stewardship, empowerment, Zen management, managing from the heart and more." Goodpaster's assessment is supported by ads for "Successories," once found in every in-flight magazine. These plaques and posters evoke a secular spirituality of idealism, perseverance, integrity, discipline and commitment. "The soul is dyed the color of its thoughts," one poster proclaims. "What you choose, what you think and what you do is who you become" says another. These slogans fall short of an authentic Catholic spirituality because they focus too much on self-reliance and stop short of grace and belief in a transcendent God. However, they are not a bad start. Our choices and our thoughts *do* shape who we become. If we become virtuous persons, then our business practices will be virtuous, as well.

In their book *Bringing Your Business to Life: The Four Virtues that will Help You Build a Better Business and a Better Life* authors Jeffrey Cornwall and Michael Naughton note the dangers of the "divided life." They say that the start of virtue is "seeing things whole." Neither the markets nor the state can create this vision. Rather, we need a strong culture which helps us see the big picture. "When culture is at its best, that is when it connects us to our created purpose, to our true nature and to our destiny, it enables us to see the whole and not merely the parts." They put the four cardinal virtues – justice, courage, prudence and temperance – at the heart of successful and fulfilling business practices.

The first step toward acquiring this virtue is to make a serious attempt to integrate our business activities with our moral and spiritual lives. More than twenty years ago, authors Richard Pascale and Tony Athos noted that Americans "have evolved a culture that separates man's spiritual life from him institutional life…Our companies freely lay claim to mind and muscle, but they are culturally discouraged from intruding upon our personal lives and deeper beliefs…"[27] It is easy to compartmentalize and see work as "just a job" that takes place from Monday through Friday, with "spirituality" reserved for Sunday morning. Business may not be explicitly religious, but it surely has a spiritual and ethical dimension. We must resist the temptation to isolate business and spirituality from one another, and make spiritual reflection an everyday event.

If we take the Incarnation seriously, we have to look for grace in every aspect of our lives. This is the difference between a job and a vocation. In a job, we work to earn a living. Our work is only a means to an end. As a vocation, however, work leads us to do everything "for the greater Glory of God." Learning to do that takes a lifetime. Once we begin to achieve it, we become different kinds of persons who are holy not in spite of, but *through* the challenges of our work.

Vocations are not fulfilled accidentally. They require serious discipline and commitment to what Gregory F. Augustine Pierce calls a "spirituality of work." His definition of a spirituality of work involves "a serious, long-term, disciplined attempt to align oneself and one's environment with transcendental reality, the ultimate meaning of existence, the holy, the divine, in a word, with God, in and through all our efforts to make the world a little better place, a little closer to the way or reign of God."[28] Far from being "just a job," this kind of spirituality makes us co-creators with God. Little by little, our efforts are blessed and perfected by grace so that they reflect God's own justice.

Pierce cites five specific disciplines that can help us shape our work into a vocation: the discipline of sacred objects (keeping beautiful and holy things close at hand to remind ourselves of the possibility of the transcendent), the discipline of living with our imperfections, the discipline of assuring quality, the discipline of giving thanks and congratulations, and the discipline of deciding what is enough...and sticking to it.

Perhaps the last discipline is the most important. The abundance in our society makes it very hard for us to set limits. There is always a bigger house, a better job, a higher salary. But the Paschal Mystery – "Christ has died, Christ is risen, Christ will come again" – reminds us that in this life, there must be a point where we say "enough," a point where we release our tight grip on our possessions and allow our souls to be satisfied by the Spirit. Especially as we pass middle age, this is the major task of spiritual maturity. If we are gracefully able to let go of our youth, our wealth, our unlimited choices, our freedom, we become holy. If not, we sink into bitterness and despair.

Vocation also requires a clear life-goal and the ability to constantly readjust our lives so that they are consistent with that goal. Catholic morality is fundamentally goal-oriented or "teleological." Rather than merely doing what we are told, our tradition teaches us that morality is an intelligent search for happiness and fulfillment. The happiness we seek is not momentary or short-term, but deep and rich. Unfortunately, we often take the easy way out and settle for less than the best. This is the essence of sin: not just breaking the law, but deliberately choosing a lesser good than we are able to choose.

Professor Goodpaster applies this goal-oriented approach to business ethics . He describes "teleopathy" or "goal sickness" as "an unbalanced pursuit of purpose" which causes our "*telos*" or life-goal to become narrow and restricted, leading us to make bad choices. Teleopathy has three symptoms: rationalization, detachment and fixation.

Rationalization is denial, reinterpretation, and selective vision that makes us see only what we want to see. This most often occurs because of exclusive loyalty to stockholders, or a kind of legality that "appeals to the permissibility of a behavior or policy within the constraints of the law." Or we can rationalize by telling ourselves that harsh practices are "just business decisions" rather than free choices of one moral good over another.

Detachment is "a kind of isolation from moral responsiveness," which causes us separate head from heart and "lose the ability to connect our behavior to the larger human picture. " Surely the executives who risked the jobs and pension funds of thousands of employees were detached from the big picture in a serious way.

We find a perfect example of rationalization and detachment in the wake of the sub-prime mortgage scandal of 2007. Members of a Congressional Commission established to determine where the fault for the crisis lay said they were shocked by the distance the bankers put between themselves and the crisis. Highly paid executives testified that they had "no idea" that these enormous risks were being created. In over 700 interviews, one member of the commission said, "not one individual linked his or her personal behavior to the crisis." [29]

Finally, Goodpaster describes *fixation* as an excessive focus on narrow, short-term goals and the "thoughtlessness or recklessness of seeking objectives whose full implications are under examined." In the case of recent corporate scandals, that goal was personal enrichment and profit understood only in terms of dollars. "Managing a corporation with the single measure of share price is like flying a 747 for maximum speed. You can shake the thing apart," says Marjorie Kelly. "It's like a farmer forcing more and more of a crop to grow, until the soil is depleted and nothing will grow." One of the necessary reforms of business is to make corporations accountable not only for shareholder profit, but for helping society to achieve other kinds of values, as well.

It is not hard to see how the subprime mortgage crisis that began in 2007 was a textbook case of teleopathy, or what some have called "short-termism." It started with overcommitment by borrowers, who wanted more real estate in the short term; it continued with banks willing to overlook borrowers' inability to pay, because they wanted more closing fees in the short term (in the mortgage business, loan underwriting became so lax that these mortgages were actually called "liar loans). The crisis expanded with securitization, because banks wanted to bundle these loans and extract profit from them as quickly as possible. Every player lost sight of the long term and opted for gains here and now.[30]

Peter O'Driscoll suggests that we can highlight these other values by rejecting the "invisible hand" argument that favors free markets and unfettered competition. Instead, he proposes a theory described as "mindful markets." Proponents of this theory say that markets should be judged not just by the amount of profit they generate, but "by their contributions to life and the maintenance of ethical culture." O'Driscoll says these ideas echo the Church's insistence on human dignity, economic justice and the linkage between the religious and social dimensions of life.

A "mindful market" urges firms to operate in ways that "allow for broad involvement in decision-making, some degree of meaningful stakeholder ownership (as opposed to the absentee shareholder model) and effective government oversight."[31] Broader involvement of stake-holders reflects the Church's tradition of subsidiarity – which seeks maximum participation by all members of society. It calls on government to organize – but not replace – the responsibility of ordinary citizens. Relying on the absolute will of a sovereign monarch might have been necessary in some eras where communication was poor and education rare. But today, electronic media allow most citizens to be well informed enough to actively participate in social decision-making. The ability to do so allows all of us to contribute to the common good.

Toward a Catholic Spirituality of Business

Pierce's definition of business spirituality as a "long term, disciplined attempt to align oneself and one's environment with transcendent reality" is an excellent basis for understanding how business people make their work a vocation, a response to their baptismal call to be followers of Jesus. We might expand on it somewhat by citing three additional elements.

Distinguishing Money and Meaning. "Our way out of the current mess requires a new seriousness about money," says Professor James E. Fisher of Saint Louis University School of Business. "People do not work primarily for money, but rather to find meaning in work that is challenging and important."[32] Money, and even profit, are not bad things. Although Catholic social teaching sets limits to income and promotes the equitable distribution of wealth, it does not prohibit the accumulation of wealth. Still, we must remember that work has a number of purposes. As John Paul II pointed out in his encyclical *Laborem Exercens*, work is one of the basic ways in which we build our lives and find fulfillment. Even menial work can be done with pride and care so that whatever we do, we do for the glory of God.

Pope Benedict XVI in his encyclical *Caritas in Veritate* addresses businesses directly. In addition to the economy of the market, he says, we must acknowledge the economy of gift – remembering that all the resources business uses were give first to all of us as a gift.

Sacramentality. Finding meaning in our work helps us see work as sacramental. Catholics of a certain age used to talk about "occasions of sin," but there are also "occasions of grace," viz., words, actions or gestures that actually make us aware of the presence of God. In addition to the seven Sacraments, which are privileged occasions of grace, there are many others as well.

These occasions can be found in our work. I think, for example, of an experience I had one day at the supermarket. We all know the scene: It was 5:30 p.m., and the express line was full of impatient shoppers. At the head of the line was an elderly woman who was attempting to pay for a few modest purchases with a combination of food stamps and cash. At one point she realized she didn't have enough cash, so she removed an item from the cart. Then she decided to replace that item, and relinquish another. When the final tally was made, she had difficulty counting out her nickels and dimes. Through all of this, the young woman cashier exercised infinite patience and grace, helping her decide what to keep and finding the right change in her coin purse. All of us standing behind her observed her kindness and generosity. We settled down and replaced our sharp, impatient glances with smiles. When at last the transaction was complete, and the elderly customer had departed, the next person in line commended the cashier. "You were wonderful with that woman," he said. We all agreed. The way the cashier did her job was sacramental. In her actions, we all saw God's own care.

Solidarity and the Common Good. Goodpaster's description of detachment militates against the notion of solidarity, which is deeply rooted in Catholic social teaching. Solidarity means simply, "we're all in this together." It means that when one of us is sick, or uneducated, or unemployed, we are all diminished. Business persons who see their work as a vocation will always try to see the whole picture, and anticipate all the consequences of their actions, not just the impact on the bottom line. It is true that without a strong balance sheet, no corporation will survive. But when businesses incorporate, they make a tacit agreement with society not only to make money, but to make society a better place to live. They agree not only to promote individual goods such as profit, but the common good.

A perfect example of this is the case of Malden Mills, which manufactures Polartec® fabric. When the Massachusetts factory burned to the ground in1995, The CEO, Aaron Feuerstein, pledged to rebuild rather than relocate and to keep paying all 3,000 employees while he did so. With the cooperation of state and local officials, the factory reopened, and the company exceeded its pre-fire levels of production and employment. Even though market changes forced Malden Mills to declare bankruptcy twice and to be absorbed by a larger corporation in 2007, Feurstein never doubted he had done the right thing. He saw his company not just as a cash register but as a social force in the life of the community.

Corporate today life is in need of redemption. Scandal has weakened business economically and has made business leaders suspect. The rich resources of our spiritual tradition can help Catholic business people lead the way in restoring respectability and making business a creative and holy calling.

Chapter 14 – Adult Morality
and the Gifts of the Holy Spirit

Most Catholics remember something about the Holy Spirit. They may have memorized the Prayer to the Holy Spirit and heard that at Confirmation the Holy Spirit made them "soldiers of Christ." They might have heard the *Veni Creator Spiritus* at an ordination or the long sequence after the first reading at Mass on the Feast of Pentecost: "Come O Holy Spirit, Come! From your bright and blissful home!" They might even recall the seven Gifts and the twelve Fruits of the Holy Spirit. Few of us, however, would think of the Gifts of the Holy Spirit as having anything to do with the moral life or the virtues. Even fewer would know that for many important theologians, including Thomas Aquinas, the Gifts of the Spirit were an indispensable part of the moral life. Yet since then, the Holy Spirit has not always gotten the attention it deserves. Fr. Kilian McDonnell says, "The Holy Spirit has had difficulty winning recognition as a full person. We think we know what a Father is, and a Son, but what is a Spirit?" He goes on to suggest that the Spirit might need some kind of "affirmative action" to help it recover its rightful place in our lives! This is all the more true in our moral lives, where the Spirit offers us special kinds of assistance.

The gifts of the Holy Spirit are important for a number of reasons. First of all, they are not divine "shocks" but qualities or "habits" which remain with us; second, they are intuitive or instinctive "promptings" which guide us through difficult and complex moral decisions after we have "thought it all out;" third, they help us see our own sinfulness and need for God's healing grace; and fourth, they provide the continuity and consistency that are the hallmark of a mature, "grown up" moral and spiritual life. Let us examine each of these benefits in more detail.

The Gifts as moral qualities: the difference between "knowing about" and "having"

Human persons have different ways of knowing things. On one level, we can consult books and through our study learn all about something. For example, I can learn about justice or chastity or kindness, but never actually practice them in my own life. I can learn about Jesus Christ, but never know him personally. I can know about racism, but still be deeply racist within. I can do something that is right because I am told to do it, but lack any inner understanding of or experience of the goodness of that act. Children, for example, can be compelled to do or not to something, but they comply grudgingly and will sometimes return to the same forbidden activity the first chance they get. "Didn't I tell you not to do that?" an exasperated parent might ask. "Yes," the child replies. But he may be too young to have understood why, or to have experienced the moral satisfaction of doing the right thing.

As we grow older, we begin to have concrete experiences of moral goodness. Once we do, we move beyond merely knowing *about* morality; we begin to experience it, and it becomes part of us. As we mature morally, moral goodness is not something we have to learn over and over. It becomes "second nature," or in theological language, "connatural." Like the pianist or the athlete who through practice are able to produce beautiful music or skillful moves with no apparent effort, as we grow older we gradually begin to absorb morality so that doing the right thing comes naturally. At this point, we don't just "know about" morality, we "have it." Once we "know" these moral truths in our very being, we begin to develop virtues – moral skills that enable us to do the right thing almost without thinking about it.

This is where the Gifts of the Holy Spirit come in. They are "connatural" too, but instead of arising from our own efforts to become good, they come directly from God. The Gifts work hand-in-hand with the virtues by strengthening them and making them more resilient. Just as the virtues lead us to a certain kind of moral perfection on a human level, the Gifts lead us further, to divine perfection that is an experience of God's own life.

The Gifts as Divine Instincts, Intuitions or "Tastes"

First referred to in Chapter 11 of the Book of Isaiah, the Gifts are seven in number: understanding, knowledge, wisdom, counsel, piety, fear and fortitude. They involve God's direct activity in our lives so that we "know" something of God's will or about God's own self from deep within ourselves. These special kinds of knowing are necessary because unlike animals or plants, human persons have a divine destiny. We were created to be with God. This means that even though we can achieve a kind of happiness in this world by living a good life, what God really has in store for us lies beyond our own abilities. The Happiness of the next world is something we cannot achieve on our own, but the Gifts of the Spirit help us see it and strive for it.

The language that theologians have used to describe the Gifts is remarkably concrete. They are described as intuitions, instincts, or even as a "taste for God." In his book *The Fruits and Gifts of the Holy Spirit* Abbot Thomas Keating asks "Is it really possible to taste God? The answer is yes, but we cannot bring it about by our own efforts." Another writer said that with the Gifts, the moral and spiritual life becomes "more...tactile, allowing for a kind of feeling, touching and tasting the divine." St. Thomas Aquinas refers to the Gifts dozens of times as "divine instincts." Describing the Gifts in this way reminds us that we have a built in sense for the Holy and that morality is not just a matter of obeying rules but of enjoying God just as we would enjoy beautiful art, good food, and the deeply satisfying pleasures of human touch. Just as God has given birds an instinctual knowledge about building nests, flying south and avoiding cats, so he has given us a supernatural instinct to know that we are made to be with him.

Assistance with Difficult and Complex Moral Choices

As our lives become more complex, so do the moral choices we face. We might be faced with a business decision, for example, that could have great financial implications for our family. Deciding to invest in this way or that, to expand our business or contract, to change jobs or stay put are all difficult moral choices that have many uncertainties. Medical problems present the same dilemma. The illness itself may be complicated and frightening, and then we are presented with range of treatment options which have side effects, some chance of failure, and many other uncertainties. Despite our best efforts, we are can be overwhelmed by the complexity of the situation and our own fears. We stumble around and make mistakes.

Just a few years ago there was a case in England of a couple that gave birth to conjoined twins, Mary and Jodie. The twins shared some vital organs, so that any attempt to separate them would result in the death of one of them. Columnist John Allen commented that the parents were faced with a "stark 'Sophie's Choice' – mark one of your children to die or they both perish."

Redemptorist Father Brian Johnstone, a moral theologian who commented on the case, said that the moral calculus in this case was so murky they were at a point "where logic can't take you any further." Yet our own uncertainty and even the limits of logic are not cause for discouragement. "This very imperfection," Dominican Father Walter Farrell wrote in his book *Swift Victory* more than 50 years ago, "is the occasion and reason for an entirely new and different series of habitual graces from the Holy Spirit – the Gifts."

In any moral decision there are always three steps. The first is to make sure we *understand the circumstances* of the moral problem clearly, because "the right question is half the answer." This seems obvious, but it is often difficult to come up with a clear picture of the actual situation, especially when we are dealing with a technical area like medicine. The second is to *think it through* as thoroughly as we can, being careful to seek counsel from those around us, especially those who are knowledgeable or who have had experiences similar to ours. And finally, when we have gained as much insight as we can from logic and clear thinking, we *pray and seek the guidance of the Spirit.* As spiritual theologian Christopher Kiesling notes, "What the Holy Spirit contributes is a perfecting of this whole process of decision making. The spirit does not substitute her activity for ours, but complements and perfects it." Once we have done all we can do on our own, the Spirit sweeps away our confusion and brings clarity. The Spirit enables us to see beyond details to the "big picture" so that we can make a peaceful and confident decision.

The Spirit Makes Us Aware of Our Own Sinfulness

The poet W.H. Auden said that "we would rather be ruined than changed; we'd rather die in our own dread than mount the cross of the moment and let our illusions die...."

Recognizing our own sinfulness, moving beyond our own limitations, is probably the most challenging aspect of growth in the spiritual life. It is not unlike 12-step programs designed for those who suffer from addiction. In order to begin the recovery process, they must first acknowledge that they are powerless and totally dependent upon God. This is what we know as the Gift of Understanding.

The American short story writer Flannery O'Connor describes this experience beautifully in a story entitled "The Artificial Nigger," in which the main character, Mr. Head, decides to take his grandson Nelson into the big city for the first time. Once there, they get lost and in the confusion, Nelson runs into a woman and knocks her down, causing her to spill her bags of groceries all over the sidewalk. In his panic and embarrassment Mr. Head denies Nelson, pretending he doesn't know him. Eventually, in a moment of insight granted by the Spirit, Mr. Head realizes what he has done. Ms. O'Connor describes the experience, using the traditional image for the Spirit, a flame:

> Mr. Head stood very still and felt the action of mercy touch him again but this time he knew that there were no words in the world that could name it. He stood appalled, judging himself with the thoroughness of God, while the action of mercy covered his pride like a flame and consumed it. He had never thought himself a great sinner before, but he saw now that his true depravity had been hidden from him lest it cause him despair. He saw that no sin was too monstrous for him to claim as his own, and since God loved in proportion as he forgave, he felt ready at that instant to enter paradise...

The remarkable thing about this Gift is that at the moment Mr. Head realized his sinfulness, he also realized the immense love and saving power of God, and knew that he was forgiven and redeemed. As Abbot Thomas notes, whether this Gift "comes through terrible suffering or develops gradually, it makes us aware that we are capable of any evil and that only God is our strength." This is not a morbid meditation our own sinfulness, but a process of awakening to the fact that, as theologian Yves Congar says, "we are not all that we should be and with God's grace could be."

The implication is that sometimes the action of the Spirit in our lives may not be entirely pleasant. As it strips us of our illusions, it may cause us a "dark night" of discouragement and depression in which have to lose our "former selves." It is a hard process, but it always leads to a new morning of grace.

Continuity and Spontaneity in the Moral Life

We sometimes have a tendency to see our moral lives as a series of unrelated snapshots – e.g., I did this right, I did this wrong, I could have done better there, I failed here. While it is true that we are faced with many discrete moral choices, it is important for us to remember that there is also an overarching flow or narrative to our moral lives. As we grow older we develop character, or virtue, so that the moral question we face is not just "What ought I to do?" but "What kind of person do I want to become?" Moral maturity means looking for patterns in our lives – good or bad. If we discern patterns of lying or dishonesty or cruelty, we need to find the actions that have shaped that kind of character and root them out. Similarly, if we are aware of moral strengths, true charity, concern, justice or chastity, we need to cultivate the behavior that has contributed to them. The Gifts are not "one-at-a-time" interventions or "sparks of Grace" in our lives, but "habitual dispositions placed in our soul which lead us easily to consent to God's inspirations."

As divine qualities, the Gifts of the Spirit take up residence in us more or less permanently. They actually "bend us toward God," so that we not only seek the good but do it readily and with pleasure. The Gifts give a "fluid mobility" to our actions so that, in the words of theologian Thomas O'Meara, we don't only live "rationally and metho-dically, but exuberantly and spontaneously."

The 17th century theologian John of St. Thomas, who is famous for his work on the Gifts of the Holy Spirit, uses a nautical image to describe this spontaneity: "Though the forward progress of the ship may be the same, there is a vast difference in its being moved by the laborious rowing of oarsmen and its being moved by sails filled with a strong breeze." So it is with the moral life. Aided by grace and the virtues, we may eventually attain a kind of human goodness; but with the Gifts of the Spirit we are moved quickly along to a Destination that we could never achieve on our own.

Perhaps the most important gift in this regard is the gift of fortitude, or courage. Although we often associate "courage" with heroes, it is in fact a very ordinary, everyday Gift that enables us to keep our "eyes on the prize." Whether it is the ordinary commitment of marriage or religious life, or the discipline of hard work or raising children, most of us need nothing more than the ability to stick to it. We need an everyday courage that enables us to get up in the morning knowing that we have certain tasks and responsibilities before us, but also that beyond those daily challenges is the destiny of eternal life that God offers us. The Gifts enable us to see that destiny clearly, to actually feel God's grace, and to continue to strive.

The best news about the Gifts of the Spirit is that as we get older, the moral life should become easier and more "second nature" to us. We no longer make the foolish, rash mistakes we did when we were young; we no longer have such short-sighted moral vision that we can only see our own needs. Even though the Gifts are given to everyone – even children – it is most often as adults that we gain the sensitivity to know they are there and take advantage of them.

In their excellent book *Conscience and Prayer: The Spirit of Catholic Moral Theology*, Redemptorist Father Dennis Billy and his colleague James Keating suggest a process of "theological reflection" that will help us cultivate sensitivity to the Gifts. This process involves several steps, including: "the connatural knowledge of contemplative prayer, the theoretical and practical insights gained from spiritual reading, the emotional experience received from a prayerful use of the imagination, the 'body knowledge' coming from such practices as fasting and abstinence and the 'sense of the faith' imbibed by immersing oneself in the liturgical traditions of the Church."

Along with clear thinking, these practices will make us more sensitive to the Gifts God is always waiting to offer and help move us to a confident, grown-up experience of the moral life.

Resources

This is a list of articles and books that will help you explore many of the topics discussed in this book in greater detail.

Catholic Moral Theology: Method and History

James F. Keenan, *A History of Catholic Moral Theology in the Twentieth Century: From Confessing Sins to Liberating Conscience.* New York: Continuum, 2010.

John Mahoney, S.J. *The Making of Moral Theology: A Study of the Roman Catholic Tradition.* New York: Oxford, 1987.

William C. Mattison. *Introducing Moral Theology: True Happiness and the Virtues.* New York: Brazos, 2008.

Kevin O'Neill, C.Ss.R. and Peter Black. *The Essential Moral Handbook: Guide to Catholic Living.* Revised Edition. Liguori Publications, 2006. An excellent, user-friendly resource that includes a glossary.

Servais Pinckaers, O.P. *Morality: The Catholic View.* South Bend, IN: St. Augustine's Press, 2003.

The Bible and Moral Theology

Benedict Ashley, OP. *Living the Truth In Love: A Biblical Introduction to Moral Theology.* New York, Alba House, 1992.

Pontifical Biblical Commission. *The Bible and Morality: Biblical Roots of Christian Conduct.* Rome, 2008.

Liturgy, Spirituality and the Moral Life

Richard Gula, SS. *The Good Life: Where Morality and Spirituality Converge.* New York: Paulist, 1999.

James Keating, SJ. Spirituality and Moral Theology: Essays from a Pastoral Perspective. New York: Paulist Press, 2000.

Alexander Lucie-Smith. "Liturgy and the Moral Life: Making the Connections." *The Heythrop Journal* (55:4) July 2012, 649-661.

The Virtues and the Moral Life

Mitch Finley. *The Catholic Virtues: Seven Pillars of a Good Life*. Liguori, MO: Liguori Publications, 1999.

James C. Mattison, *Introducing Moral Theology: True Happiness and the Virtues*. "Chapter 3, "Why Virtue? Morality is More Than Actions."

Scott Bader-Saye. *Following Jesus in a Culture of Fear*. New York: Brazos, 2007.

Paul Waddell. *The Primacy of Love: An Introduction to the Ethics of Thomas Aquinas*. New York: Paulist, 1992. Even though it is currently out of print, this is perhaps the best introduction to the heart of Thomas Aquinas' ethics with an emphasis on virtue and friendship.

Health Care Ethics

Benedict Ashley, O.P., Jean de Blois, C.S.J., and Kevin O'Rourke, O.P. *Health Care Ethics: A Catholic Theological Analysis*. 5th Edition. Washington: Georgetown University Press, 2006. This is still the standard textbook for Catholic health care ethics. For a more concise version, see Ashley and O'Rourke's *Ethics of Health Care: An Introductory Textbook* (Washington, Georgetown, 2002).

Kevin D. O'Rourke and Philip J. Boyle. *Medical Ethics: Sources of Catholic Teaching*. 5th Edition. Washington: Georgetown University Press, 2011. This is an excellent reference for students, pastors, health care providers and patients who want to know where specific teachings are found in Church documents.

Michael Panicola et al., *Health Care Ethics: Theological Foundations, Contemporary Issues, and Controversial Cases*. Winona, MN: Anselm Academic, 2011.

The Gifts of the Holy Spirit

Benedict Ashley, O.P. *Thomas Aquinas: The Gifts of the Holy Spirit*. Hyde Park, NY: New City Press, 1995.

Thomas Keating, OCSO. *The Fruits and Gifts of the Holy Spirit*. New York: Lantern Books, 2007.

Christopher Kiesling, O.P. "The Seven Quiet Gifts of the Holy Spirit." *Living Light* 23(1986): 137-50.

John Mahoney, S.J. "The Spirit and Moral Discernment in Aquinas," and "The Spirit and Community Discernment in Aquinas," and *Seeking the Spirit: Essays in Moral and Pastoral Theology* (Denville, NJ: Dimension Books, 1981).

Business Ethics

Helen Alford, O.P., and Michael Naughton. *Managing As If Faith Mattered: Christian Social Principles in the Modern Organization.* Notre Dame: University of Notre Dame Press, 2001. This is an excellent application of Catholic social teaching to contemporary business.

Jeffrey Cornwall and Michael Naughton. *Bringing Your Business To Life: The Four Virtues That Will Help You Build a Better Business and a Better Life.* Ventura CA: Regal, 2008. A very accessible volume written to help entrepreneurs build virtuous businesses.

Kenneth E. Goodpaster. *Conscience and Corporate Culture.* Malden, MA: Blackwell Publishing, 2007.

John C. Médaille. *The Vocation of Business: Social Justice in the Marketplace.* New York: Continuum, 2011.

James L. Nolan. *Doing the Right Thing at Work: A Catholic's Guide to Faith, Business And Ethics.* Cincinnati: Franciscan Media, 2005.

Sexual Ethics

Vincent Genovesi. *In Pursuit of Love: Catholic Morality and Human Sexuality.* Second Edition. Collegeville: Liturgical Press/Michael Glazier, 1996.

John Grabowski. *Sex and Virtue: An Introduction to Sexual Ethics.* Washington: Catholic University of America Press, 2003.

Todd Salzman and Michael Lawler. *Sexual Ethics: A Theological Introduction.* Washington: Georgetown University Press, 2012.

Notes

---

[1]See Lisa Fulham, "Thou Shalt: Sex Beyond the List of Don'ts". *Commonweal* (April 20, 2009) for a description of this problem as well as her discussion of a positive, virtue-based approach.

[2]See William Cosgrove, "How Celtic Penance Gave us Personal Confession," *Doctrine and Life* 41(October 1991): 412-422.

[3]*The Responsible Christian: A Popular Guide for Moral Decision Making According to Classical Tradition.* Chicago: Loyola University Press, 1984.

[4]William Pfaff, "The Pope Identifies American Problem," *Los Angeles Times,* October 1, 1993.

[5]Peter Steinfels, "Beliefs," *The New York Times,* October 16, 1993.

[6]Servais Pinckaers, O.P. "Virtue is Not a Habit." *Cross Currents* (Winter 1962): 65-79.

[7] Scott Shane, "A Year of Terror Plots Through a Second Prism." *New York Times,* January 13, 2010

[8] The Kaiser Family Foundation provides a wealth of comparative health care data in very accessible form. See www.kff.org

[9] "America's Blind Spot: Health Care and the Common Good." *Commonweal* (October 9, 2009).

[10] Stephen Boren and David Boren, "What is Rationing?" *New England Journal of Medicine* (41:213) July 15, 1999.

[11] "The Cost is Too High, The Loss is Too Great," March 15, 2010.

[12]Daniel Callahan, "High Tech or Long-Term Care? Let the Elderly Decide." *New York Times* (June 12, 1994): 15.

[13]Norman Paradis, "Making a Living Off the Dying." *New York Times* (June 12, 1994).

[14]Philip Keane, *Health Care Reform: A Catholic Perspective.* New York: Paulist 1993.

[15]St. Thomas Aquinas, *Summa Theologica,* 1-2, q. 96, a. 2. Cited in *Evangelium Vitae,* #71, note 92.

[16] St. Thomas cites Augustine's opinion in this matter in ST 2-2, q. 10, a. 12: "Thus Augustine says, 'if you do away with harlots the world will be convulsed with lust. Hence, though unbelievers sin in their rites, they be be tolerated, either on account of some good that ensues, or because of some evil avoided (e.g., scandal or disturbance)."

[17]"[Political] dominion would have existed in the state of innocence for two reasons: first of all because we are naturally social...and the social life of many is not possible unless someone presides who can direct the group toward the common good... Second, because if one man greatly surpassed another in knowledge and justice, it would be all wrong if he did not perform this function for the benefit of others..." (ST I, q. 96, a. 4.)

[18]Frank Nichols, "Sexuality Fully Human," *The Furrow* (March 1983): 145-154.

[19]Bernard Haring, *Free and Faithful in Christ: Moral Theology for Clergy and Laity*. 3 volumes. New York: Crossroad, 1981. 2:504.

[20]Congregation for the Doctrine of the Faith, "The Pastoral Care of Homosexual Persons," October 1, 1986, #16.

[21]Philip Keane, *Sexual Morality: A Catholic Perspective*. New York, Paulist, 1977, p. 65.

[22]"Doing Sexual Ethics in a Post-Permissive Society," *The Way* 28(1988): 244ff

[23]Andre Guindon, *The Sexual Creators: An Ethical Proposal for Concerned Christians*. Lanham, MD: The University Press of America, 1986. See Chapter 4, "Toward a Renewed Notion of Sexual Fecundity."

[24]Ronald Lawler, Joseph Boyle and William May, *Catholic Sexual Ethics: A Summary, Explanation and Defense*. Second Edition (Huntington, Indiana: Our Sunday Visitor, 1998): 125-26.

[25]Vigen Guroian, *Incarnate Love: Essays in Orthodox Ethics*. (Notre Dame, 1987). See especially Chapter 4, "An Ethic of Marriage and Family."

[26] Louis Lavelle, "Executive Pay." *Business Week Online* (April 15, 2002).

[27] The Art of Japanese Management," 1981. Quoted in Goodpaster, "Work, Spirituality and the Moral Point of View," *International Journal of Value Based Management7*(1994): 49-62.

[28] Gregory F. Augustine Pierce, "Disciplines for a Spirituality of Work," *Origins* 28 (January 28, 1999) 550-545.

[29] National Public Radio's "Planet Money" aired a discussion entitled "The Moral of the Financial Crisis" on January 28, 2011. They describe the work of the Congressional Commission whose purpose was to find the causes of the banking crisis.

[30] CNBC's June, 2009 documentary "House of Cards" presents one hypothesis about how these factors converged to create one of the worst economic crises in the country's history.

[31]"Catholic Social Teaching and Mindful Markets," *America* January 7-14, 2002, 12-14.

127

32 "The Stock Market – How Do We Turn it Around?" *St. Louis Post-Dispatch* (July 30, 2002)

Made in the USA
Charleston, SC
26 January 2015